THE EXCHANGE STRATEGY FOR
MANAGING
CONFLICT
IN HEALTH CARE

THE EXCHANGE STRATEGY FOR

MANAGING CONFLICT

IN HEALTH CARE

How to Defuse Emotions and Create Solutions When the Stakes Are High

STEVEN P. DINKIN

BARBARA FILNER

LISA MAXWELL

New York Chicago San Francisco Lisbon London Madrid Mexico City
Milan New Delhi San Juan Seoul Singapore Sydney Toronto

The **McGraw·Hill** Companies

Copyright © 2013 by National Conflict Resource Center. All rights reserved. Printed in the United States of America. Except as permitted under the United States Copyright Act of 1976, no part of this publication may be reproduced or distributed in any form or by any means, or stored in a data base or retrieval system, without prior written permission of the publisher.

1 2 3 4 5 6 7 8 9 0   DOC/DOC   1 8 7 6 5 4 3 2

ISBN   978-0-07-180196-6
MHID   0-07-180196-0

e-ISBN   978-0-07-180197-3
e-MHID   0-07-180197-9

McGraw-Hill books are available at special quantity discounts to use as premiums and sales promotions, or for use in corporate training programs. To contact a representative, please e-mail us at bulksales@mcgraw-hill.com.

This book is printed on acid-free paper.

To healthcare providers
for the benefit of patients and their families

Contents

Acknowledgments

Our thanks to the following people who helped us in the writing of this book:

Nora Jaffe, member of NCRC's board of directors, and **Barbara Lee**, a friend and participant in an Exchange training, reviewed and commented upon an early draft of this book. We are grateful for their time and editing skills.

Robin Seigle, Director of NCRC's Business Division, was our best proofreader. She found many typos and misused words, and had a sharp eye for many other details.

Leneah Manuma, NCRC Training Institute Administrative Assistant worked to finish the details required for the manuscript to be submitted.

The NCRC staff believed in us from the very beginning. At times they did extra office chores; at other times they stayed out of the way so the three of us could meet. We could not ask for a better team.

NCRC volunteer mediators, credentialing candidates, and panel specialists contributed cases, comments, and care for nearly 30 years. Without them there would be no book.

PRINCIPLED NEGOTIATION AND MEDIATION

Although The Exchange is unique in its structure, it reflects important principles from many sources, especially principled negotiation and mediation. Principled negotiation, developed in Roger Fisher and William Ury's book, *Getting to Yes*, stresses that in order to be successful, negotiators need to recognize each other's interests—and to realize that their interests are interconnected. Mediation is built on empowerment, respect, and an awareness that its results affect far more people than the individuals who are directly involved.

Foreword

Health care is a high-stakes business. Whether you work for a hospital, a doctor's office, or some other healthcare facility, you know people's lives are on the line every day. Failure is *not* an option. And the pressure to succeed combined with the stress of caring for patients and families, the regulations you must meet, and the many other challenges healthcare professionals face can lead to a big problem, *conflict*.

The impact of conflict gets expressed in many ways:

▶ A domineering, controlling administrator criticizes others in public settings.
  The Outcome: A crippling of creative thinking. Why bother?

▶ Nurses argue about protocol at the bedside of a dying patient.
  The Outcome: Increased anxiety about the end of life for the patient, loss of confidence by the family, fractured treatment.

▶ A physician's assistant leaves incomplete notes in the patient's chart.
  The Outcome: Potential patient harm; increased exposure to malpractice liability; extra time and effort are required to provide the best care.

▶ Members of a surgical team don't communicate clearly or at all.
  The Outcome: Compromised patient care.

The healthcare industry is currently under a microscope. As if the pressure and demands of new technology, sicker patients, and growing bureaucracy are not enough, everyone has become an instant expert on how to "fix" the system. It's no surprise that healthcare workers may be feeling more tension or experiencing more conflicts. The system is changing. One critical difference, however, between providers who consistently deliver high-quality care with high ratings for patient safety and those who don't is how quickly and how effectively they acknowledge problems or conflicts and how they choose to address them. If not addressed early and productively, the outcome of these ignored conflicts can be detrimental to patients, families, physicians, staff, and the organization.

> *It's not fair!*
> *Don't tell her I told you, but she . . .*
> *I can't work with him!*
> *She yelled at me in front of patients!*

What is a manager to do when he or she hears these complaints from staff? Though a natural reaction is to either simply avoid the complaints altogether or tell employees to go back to work, neither of these approaches tend to work very well. What most managers want is for their staff to treat each other with respect, work cooperatively, and focus on excellent patient care.

The question is how can an organization create a positive work environment and help channel the staff's energy toward contributing, instead of petty infighting or other disruptive behavior. One thing is known to be true—the more a manager ignores or tries to squash the problem, the more it tends to escalate and the more complaining increases. As a French philosopher once said, "Everything has been said before, but since no one listens, we have to begin all over again." Employees, like most other people, don't like to be ignored or told their concerns and reactions to a situation are wrong, bad, or inappropriate.

In the busy reality of delivering patient care, it may feel as though one does not have time to manage a conflict or to listen to employees' concerns. The cost of not listening to employees' concerns is great: escalation of issues, avoidance of other staff with whom they have a conflict, increased absenteeism, losing focus at work, and possibly patient harm; all of these are real consequences of workplace conflict.

Finding a way to respond respectfully and to hear the underlying interests, instead of focusing on the complaints, takes practice. What these skills can do is transform the workplace into one in which people work collaboratively and respectfully together. Having a structured conflict management strategy is an essential leadership tool which can also transform a dysfunctional team to a thriving one.

The Exchange Strategy for Managing Conflict in Health Care supports managers and supervisors, at every level of the organization, in the challenging work of managing conflict and disruptive behavior in the workplace. Fortunately, most employees do the right thing and are committed to improving, so the atmosphere is generally professional and positive. But even the best employees can sometimes find themselves in workplace conflicts for which they could use some help. Given that fact, many organizations have embarked on this training and support it for good reason:

▸ Ignoring the problem does not solve it. In fact, it exacerbates the problem. The employees in conflict (or the employee who creates a "toxic environment" in the workplace) can create a negative atmosphere for their coworkers and even impact patient care.

▸ High turnover rates are costly. When more people are let go from their jobs because of behavioral problems than competency issues, the cost to the organization is great and can be prevented in many cases.

▸ The Joint Commission is mandating that hospitals manage conflict in a way that healthcare safety and quality are protected (Standard LD.2.40). Additionally, leaders are to create a culture of safety, based on teamwork and respect, which means disruptive behavior by individuals must be addressed (Standard LD.03.01.01).

The Exchange program is based on state of the art methodology for managing conflict productively and respectfully. Combining the tools of leadership, adherence to policy, and working from an interest-based perspective, managers learn how to work through the inevitable issues that arise in the workplace. As one manager stated, *"I thought that I was going to learn about conflict management, but I have learned good tips for communicating better with my staff on an ongoing basis."*

Successful management of conflicts and disruptive behavior helps the overall mission, vision, and values of any organization. It also helps one reduce stress, manage in a more positive manner, and see other positive outcomes for employees.

The Exchange program can help create a safe, efficient, smooth-running organization. Over the past 12 months, over 450 managers and supervisors on my team at Sanford Health have gone through this training, and it works! The healthcare industry has needed a strategic process like The Exchange for many years, and I am relieved to know that we finally have a professional, well-organized process to refer to when conflicts arise in our hospitals and clinics. The Exchange is all about results. Use it at your organization and be prepared to see more efficient, less stressed employees, and, most importantly, happier, healthier patients.

Evan Burkett
CHIEF HUMAN RESOURCES OFFICER, SANFORD HEALTH

PART ONE | # Introductions

1

Welcome to The Exchange at St. Sonia's

R adha Samson reached for the phone at her desk, pushed the extension button for Drew Thompson, the head of Employee Relations at St. Sonia's Hospital, and said, "Hey, Drew, I've got another Exchange job for you. You need to get on it ASAP! Dr. Phillips called me just now to complain. One of his patients was upset by a 'fight' between two nurses. He claims it's a patient safety situation. Apparently, the elderly woman he's been working with had an alarming rise in her blood pressure when she heard her favorite nurse, RN Simon Peters, being berated by RN Yvette Jones. Naturally, he wants someone fired. I calmed him down by assuring him we'd set up an Exchange process. While he's a little skeptical, apparently he's heard enough about it to be at least momentarily satisfied. He's a great doctor—apparently he relates well with his patients—but his relations with the staff need some work, and I'd like to keep this situation from becoming worse. He had already talked to the nursing manager to complain but he wasn't sure she would take care of it, despite the fact that she said she would. I'd really like to settle this at the lowest level possible."

Drew Johnson responded, "Hmm, that would be Kim Brown. She is very clear about patient care as well as nursing standards for the nurses on the floor. Whatever he might think, she's a very good nurse manager. She hasn't yet facilitated a full Exchange process, but she did cofacilitate one with me, and she did a great job. And she has a good way with her staff. They respect her and if she wants them to meet, they'll meet. Can you give me some more details?"

Radha replied, "I don't know a whole lot, but apparently Yvette Jones and Simon Peters are involved, and they have a history of not getting along. This actually sounds like a perfect scenario for The Exchange. I'm so glad that we had most of our supervisors and managers take part in that training last fall."

Drew sighed and said, "Okay, I'll call Kim as soon as we hang up and see what I can find out. I'll let you know how it goes."

Radha ended the conversation, "Thanks, Drew. And good luck!"

After hanging up with Radha, Drew took a deep breath and decided that rather than call the nurse manager, Kim, about the incident, he would walk over to her office and talk to her. He wanted to make sure that Kim felt supported and knew that he was willing to coach her if there were difficulties.

Kim Brown, Head Nurse in Geriatrics, was responsible for everything that happened on her floor of the hospital, especially the work and interactions among the nurses. Because of her competence, as well as her personal skills, she had earned the respect of both patients and nurses, who felt free to come to her with their problems. When she had called the patient, Alma Cruz, to get more details concerning this latest complaint, the nurses' argument, she realized that something would have to be done about this long-simmering personality conflict.

When Kim saw Drew come into her office, she realized that the conflict was affecting more than just one patient and one floor of the hospital. Before he had a chance to say anything, Kim said, "I bet I know why you're here, Drew. Did Dr. Phillips call you too? I am going to conduct The Exchange with these two nurses, but I would really appreciate your support in this. I don't feel completely confident with The Exchange process yet, even though I know it works."

Drew replied, "Kim, I came specifically to assure you that I am glad to help. In fact, I told Radha that I could function as coach and we could talk as the process unfolds. I'm relieved that you have already thought about this and I agree that on first glance, The Exchange sounds like the perfect vehicle. So what do you know about the conflict?"

Kim began, "So Radha already knows about this? I suppose Dr. Phillips called her?"

Drew responded, "Good guess. You know Dr. Phillips. He's quick to advocate for his patients, which is great. And he always goes straight to the top and to every other position he thinks might help. Let's just say he covered his bases on this one."

Kim grimaced and said, "Yeah, I know. But I still wish he had stopped with me. I told him I would take care of it."

Drew wanted to remain positive, so he didn't respond to the last comment. Instead, he asked, "So what's the story? What have you heard?"

Kim filled Drew in, "Well, apparently, yesterday, Alma Cruz, who is one of Dr. Phillips's heart patients, heard two nurses arguing loudly right outside her room. She's particularly fond of Simon Peters and believed that another nurse was unfairly accusing him of giving inadequate care or something. Alma has very high blood pressure and this is what alarmed Dr. Phillips. He noticed a spike in her pressure when he was checking her during his rounds, and he came right over to complain. I've since found out that my hunch was right that the other nurse involved was Yvette Jones. Both Simon and Yvette are excellent nurses but have very, very different personalities. I guess Yvette was irritated by what she considers Simon's inability to separate himself professionally from his patients. I don't know what else. But I'll find out when I meet with each of them each for Stage One in about a half hour. Your timing is amazing, Drew. Can I check in with you after I meet with them?"

CHAPTER 2

The Exchange: A Proven Approach to Conflict Resolution

At St. Sonia's Hospital, The Exchange process is a key part of their *Integrated Conflict Management System (ICMS)*. For those unfamiliar with the concept of ICMS, it is a graduated system for addressing conflicts. At its lowest level, only the disputing parties are involved. Individuals are encouraged to make an effort to speak to the person they perceive has offended them. Because of this, many organizations that have an ICMS system of conflict resolution offer communication skills workshops so employees can gain skills in giving and receiving effective feedback.

If the one-on-one discussion is not successful or is not attempted, people can contact their supervisor or manager, who then can convene and facilitate an Exchange process. The Exchange is an ideal process for the next step. At times, neither employee has initiated a conflict resolution process but the manager sees a need to convene one. Most disputes are resolved at this point, but there are other levels available should they be needed, including professional mediation by an outside neutral.

Many healthcare facilities, as well as corporate businesses, schools, and other institutions, have adopted such a system as a way to manage the conflicts that occur in every workplace. We're talking about the kinds of conflicts that, if not addressed, result in enormous costs, both financial and personal. Unaddressed conflicts or mismanaged conflict resolution procedures result in high staff turnover, low morale, and expenses associated with litigation, which in turn lead to a poor work product and an unacceptable bottom line.

In the healthcare industry, the fundamental concern of patient safety may be threatened by these conflicts. There have been studies to indicate that these conflicts, which are most often rooted in miscommunication or lack of communication, can even lead to medical mistakes. When human beings are involved, accidents and resulting errors will always happen, but some errors are not accidents. Errors caused by lack of a clear understanding of what is needed or by the inability of individuals to speak up constructively for themselves in an inherently hierarchical culture are not inevitable. It is possible to greatly reduce the occurrence of errors by introducing new protocols of respectful communication, together with new processes that deal with conflicts stemming from communication failures. The Exchange, including the techniques it utilizes, is one of those processes; it empowers employees, at all levels, and has had demonstrable success.

In recognition of the importance of managing conflict, in 2009 the Joint Commission, an independent, not-for-profit organization that accredits and certifies healthcare organizations and programs in the United States, issued recommendations that have been heralded and implemented by conscientious healthcare providers throughout the country (see Appendix B). St Sonia's is no exception.

The good news is that chronic, low-level conflicts *can* be dealt with respectfully and successfully. There is dignity and self-respect in dealing with an issue and speaking up for oneself through a structured process that is balanced, fair, and learnable. We call that structured process The Exchange. We have found it works in a variety of situations, from a manager and two employees, to inter- and intradepartmental disputes, to one-on-one situations of disruptive employees (or bosses), and even to personal burnout. The techniques also work with spouses, partners, and kids! If The Exchange sounds like magic, be assured that it isn't. The skills take practice to master. The structure requires focus. Above all, the participants have to demonstrate at least a modicum of good faith as they work to address the issues that are part of the conflict.

THE INSPIRATION

The idea of The Exchange originated with the National Conflict Resolution Center (NCRC) in San Diego, California, which for many years focused solely on mediation. In 1983, NCRC, as the San Diego Mediation Center, developed an internationally recognized structure for the practice of mediation. While there are many models, *mediation* is essentially a process whereby an *outside neutral*—someone without a personal stake in the outcome—sits down with disputing parties and works with them to develop an agreement or settlement that everyone can live with. Mediation sessions typically last from two hours to several days. Professional mediators have years of training and experience to master their skills.

Key to the NCRC mediation model is *Stage Three*. It consists of a conversation, carefully structured by the mediator, between the disputing parties. It is truly an "exchange" on several levels:

1. First, it includes an *exchange of information*—what the "facts" are from each person's point of view.

2. Then, the mediator helps the parties in an *exchange of understanding*. This is critical and is at the heart of making real resolution possible. The idea is for each party to understand the impact of the conflict on the other—*how* the conflict has affected each person. At this point, the focus is not yet on agreement. Instead it is on understanding and acceptance that each party was affected.

3. Next, is an opportunity for an *exchange of expectations*—what action or reaction did each party hope for or want in the situation that occurred.

4. Finally, there is an *exchange of ideas* on how to resolve or handle the conflict.

The NCRC's mediation trainers have recognized over the years that it is not necessary to be a professional mediator to make use of the key communication skills of good mediators, skills that are most clearly demonstrated during the "*exchange*" stage of a mediation. These skills are ones that can be taught and learned by most individuals who are interested in learning them. Further, not everyone is in a position to be perceived as "neutral." The requirement for developing the skills to be neutral is the ability to withhold judgment and to actually listen to how others perceive a situation. The skills can be used effectively even by those who have a stake in the outcome of a situation. From this recognition came the idea of taking the skills of mediators into workplaces and into the community in the form of a new process called The Exchange.

The NCRC has also been inspired by working with good managers in all industries. Many successful managers:

▶ Demonstrate their *power* through good leadership skills.

▶ Utilize a command of workplace *rights* by fairly enforcing policies.

▶ Care enough about their staff to take into consideration the employees' workplace *interests* in the problem-solving process.

This deft use of three approaches to resolving conflicts (power, rights, and interests), as described by Harvard negotiators Roger Fisher and William Ury in their seminal work, *Getting to Yes: Negotiating Agreement Without Giving In*, are not easy to keep in balance. Yet, in settling workplace conflicts, unlike in pure negotiation or facilitative mediation, managers have the responsibility to utilize all three approaches as they manage their departments, depending on the situation that has arisen. We are impressed with those managers who have shown us that it is not only possible, but also highly beneficial, to strategically utilize power, rights, and interests successfully. The Exchange approach helps managers learn to balance these three elements and to emulate the successful managers we have observed.

Because so many levels of interaction exist in healthcare and so many different professional skills are involved, the healthcare industry is a perfect setting for The Exchange. Physicians, nursing staff, technicians, administrators, aides, cafeteria workers, support staff, and others all require different training, use different technical or professional "languages" to communicate, and have different expectations and ideas about each other. Added to the mix is the actual work of health care—the healing of patients who, with their families, have their own expectations. Then there is the innate hierarchy present in most medical facilities. All of this makes fertile ground for misunderstandings and for conflicts. Hospital leadership teams are in an excellent position to qualify as conflict managers because they are the ones to whom others complain and who, by virtue of their positions, are most often held responsible.

THE BOOK

This book is written for all those in the healthcare industry who are involved in resolving conflict, at all management levels of the organization, as well as for those who are dealing directly with patients and their families. In Part Two of the book, we will describe the techniques and the steps of the process. In Part Three, we will describe various situations in which The Exchange and the skills involved can be used to address a variety of situations; all are set at St. Sonia's Hospital, but they are common in any healthcare facility. In Part Four, we will describe how the techniques of The Exchange can be used outside of the workplace.

We have found that healthcare professionals are like professionals in other fields—their training typically did not include training in conflict management. The sad truth is that those most skilled in their professional jobs are not necessarily skilled in dealing with colleagues, employees, supervisors, or others. And, as has been widely recognized, many healthcare professionals are trained to be successful—too much depends on their success for it to be any other way—and so it is particularly difficult for them to acknowledge performance that is less than perfect.

The fact is that conflict is inevitable if people are working together. But this is not necessarily negative. At its best, conflict can be seen as a necessary component of growth and change; at its worst, conflict can escalate in a healthcare setting, resulting in spiraling litigation, pervasive low morale, and a perception of lower patient safety. Conflict is not about professional proficiency or training; it is about the reality of being human.

It is the personal level that is the central theme of this book. With almost 75 cumulative years of studying and working with conflict resolution, the authors have had experience with many different conflicts and the possibilities that exist for non-adversarial resolution.

We know that there are circumstances in which conflicts will certainly escalate. When individuals feel threatened or in danger of losing face they invariably become defensive and instinctively wish to retaliate or withdraw from the conflict situation. From our experience as mediators, trainers, and managers, we have developed a systematic way to address conflicts at their earliest level. We know that people want to be treated fairly and they want to know that they are respected, not only for their skills but also for their personhood. The Exchange process allows people to participate in problem solving in ways that preserve their dignity and give them input into decisions that affect their lives.

THE STRATEGY

The strategy of The Exchange is based on the best thinking about conflict resolution, from Sun Tsu, the mythical Chinese warrior chief (who believed that the best wars were those that weren't fought because they were resolved before they did damage), to more modern thinkers, like the aforementioned Fisher and Ury, authors of *Getting to Yes*.

The Exchange is both *a process* and *a set of techniques* that good conflict resolvers use in a variety of situations. In combination, they become a remarkable method for enhancing relationships, both professional and personal. The techniques are used in each stage of the process and each stage builds momentum toward finding the best solutions for dealing with the complexity of our workplaces. Even more importantly, those agreements or settlements tend to be upheld by the participants in greater numbers than solutions that are handed down from "above," whether by a boss, a disciplinary committee, or even a parent. The Exchange process provides one more strategy, and the techniques involved are additional tools to enhance your effectiveness in these roles. In fact, organizations find utilizing The Exchange the perfect first intervention for dealing with disruptive employees or unresolved conflicts among staff members. Rather than ignoring a situation until it gets out of control, and then pushing progressive discipline, The Exchange allows managers to deal with a problem when "it is big enough to see, yet small enough to solve," as Mike Leavitt, former Secretary of Health and Human Services, once quipped (Mike Leavitt, Oral remarks at Medicare Commission meeting, 2005).

For this prediscipline, inclusive approach, The Exchange has the support of union leadership where it has been implemented.

THE SKILLS

The Exchange process makes use of several essential techniques for effective communication and problem solving. They involve three deceptively simple tasks, each of which we will describe and analyze:

▶ Listening effectively

▶ Responding respectfully

▶ Going deeper by asking questions

These are skills that most people can learn and that are helpful in ways that go beyond conflict management in formal, structured workplace settings; they can be used in personal interactions and ordinary conversations. Many individuals have commented to us that using the skills has made a difference in their personal and professional lives. We make no promises but we do encourage you to try the techniques. More details about specific techniques are included in Appendix A, "Communication Skills for The Exchange."

THE FOUR-STEP PROCESS

There are four steps to using a formal Exchange process. Each is important and can be implemented flexibly. We'll detail each step and illustrate its importance in a healthcare institution. Figure 2.1 provides a brief description of The Exchange process.

▶ **Stage One.** This is the data-gathering stage for the manager or facilitator of the process. Its structure is a private, one-on-one meeting with each party in the identified conflict. It is an opportunity to hear, in a safe setting, how each individual perceives the situation and to let each one know what will follow as the process unwinds.

FIGURE 2.1 | OVERVIEW OF THE EXCHANGE PROCESS

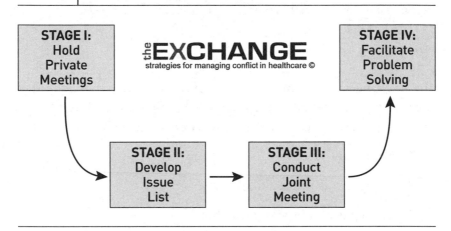

▶ *Stage Two.* This is the private-planning stage for the facilitator for developing an agenda. It may take a while when you first begin to use The Exchange, but you will find that the more you use it, the less time it will take because you will find yourself listening to participants in a different way.

▶ *Stage Three.* This is a meeting with all the participants from Stage One. The facilitator uses the agenda constructed in Stage Two to conduct a strategic three-way discussion with the goal of increasing each party's understanding, not only of his or her own role but of how the other party sees the situation.

▶ *Stage Four.* This is the problem-solving stage in which everyone participates to explore options and develop a lasting solution to the situation. Stage Three leads in and out of Stage Four.

Chapter 7 describes the classic Exchange between two employees and their manager. In the remaining chapters of Part Three, you will see how this basic process has been adapted to fit the needs of a variety of additional circumstances. We hope this book will prove useful as you do your important work in health care.

PART TWO

The Four-Stage Exchange Model

3

The Exchange, Stage One:
The Private Meetings

Before trying to find a solution to the conflict between her two nurses, Yvette Jones and Simon Peters, Kim Brown, the head nurse of geriatrics, needed to know what was going on for each of them. She would learn this by implementing Stage One of The Exchange. The essence of this stage is a private meeting with each individual. A simple enough task, yet there are important details to keep in mind as one meets with the employees individually. We will give a detailed description below of Kim's meetings with Yvette and Simon. Before that, it would be helpful to look at the fine points of Stage One.

STAGE ONE IN GREATER DETAIL

In order to create the type of environment that encourages employees to feel comfortable and facilitates real progress, managers are advised to consider the tone of the meeting. If the manager is busy looking at his or her computer, is rushing through the meeting, or is somehow distracted, this will be abundantly clear to the employee. The message will be that the manager is giving lip service to the process or to listening to the employee, but doesn't care to really engage. Managers who use the process successfully create a *tone of respectful engagement* and *really listen* to the employee's concerns. Typically, managers take about 10 to 15 minutes to conduct Stage One with each employee. This is long enough to get a picture of the situation from the person's viewpoint and short enough to keep it professional and efficient. Employees may have a fear of the joint meeting to come, so the more the manager is able to lower the anxiety level of each employee, the better the outcome will be when the two employees meet together. One manager who finds the process useful for her team tells employees:

> *Since we work in an intense environment, it is only natural that we encounter bumps (or "hiccups") in the road occasionally. We are just going to figure it out like we do everything else.*

She believes that by normalizing the conversation, it helps her employees to see it as part of what needs to happen in a successful organization.

The manager sets the tone by opening the meeting with a quick description of what the meeting is about (sometimes it will be obvious because of an incident). The manager then:

▸ Describes how the process will work. (*"I am meeting with you and I will meet with Yvette; then we will all meet together to work through the issues."*)

▸ Lets the employee know the goal of the process. (*"My goal is for the two of you to have a respectful working relationship."*)

▸ Reassures the employee about confidentiality.

Managers often know personal facts about an employee that cannot be shared with others. The manager needs to keep confidential any personal issues, concerns, or data. Sometimes this type of information or feelings about another employee may be expressed in this private meeting. Because of the nature of the work relationship, it is essential that these points are kept confidential. So, one aspect of the private meeting is to assure the employees that any personal or private information that they share will be kept in confidence. Knowing this will encourage employees to be more forthcoming regarding how the situation is affecting them in the workplace, so that the manager can construct a full picture of the situation from each person's perspective.

It is also important for the manager to distinguish personal and confidential information from issues of company policy violations or other workplace expectations. The manager has a clear responsibility to reinforce workplace policies and behavior. It works well in most situations to state clearly that the meeting is not a disciplinary session but instead is an opportunity to improve the working relationship between the two employees, and that the manager will keep private information confidential while reinforcing workplace policies and expectations.

After opening with all of this background information (usually about three minutes of talking by the manager), the manager then needs to take on a somewhat different role—that of a listener. Rather than direct the interaction, the manager should focus on listening by asking *open questions*, questions that can't be answered in one or two words. Then the manager should stop talking. The manager is listening for topics or themes of discussion. He or she is not there to convey one employee's point of view to the other employee.

Be genuinely curious as you listen. Don't give in to the temptation of offering a quick fix to the solution. Not all managers are accustomed to doing this, so it takes practice. But it is key to actually engaging the employees to participate in the problem-solving process to come. If the manager listens only long enough to hear what needs fixing, both the process and the employees' ability to come up with solutions together will be shortchanged. At this point, there is still the other *half* of the situation to learn about, so the solutions that might be suggested now would tend to be biased and shortsighted.

There may be some pieces that need to be interjected or clarified: a policy issue here, a department procedure there. Issues of the employees' working relationship and the sense that each might have that the other is being unfair or disrespectful cannot truly be resolved by the manager by edict. If the manager can listen for the underlying workplace needs and interests of each employee, he or she can go a long way toward encouraging solutions that create a better work environment for everyone.

Not surprisingly, the common workplace interests that are encountered in healthcare settings include:

▸ Respectful treatment

▸ Acceptance of different work styles

- ▸ Fairness

- ▸ Acknowledgment for contributions

- ▸ Safe work environment

- ▸ Patient safety

- ▸ Trust

- ▸ Teamwork

- ▸ Fair workload

This focused, respectful listening is further explained in Appendix A, which is well worth reviewing if you want to improve your skills in this area.

After getting a clear understanding of the situation from the first staff person's perspective, the manager closes this meeting, reinforcing the interests of the department. The manager asks the employee to be prepared to bring forward suggestions to improve the situation in the joint meeting to come, specifically ideas about what that person can do to improve things, not what he or she thinks the other employee should do. It takes just 10 to 15 minutes. There is no solution yet, but there is true buy-in and a greater sense of respect from your employee for your skills as a manager.

KIM BROWN'S PRIVATE MEETINGS WITH RN SIMON PETERS AND RN YVETTE JONES

Below, let's take a look at how Kim handles the individual meetings with RN Simon Peters and RN Yvette Jones, with additional tips given along the way.

KIM BROWN'S PRIVATE MEETING WITH RN SIMON PETERS

After checking both of their schedules, Kim decides to start with RN Simon Peters. This is what transpires during their private meeting:

Simon, thank you for coming in. I won't beat around the bush, you know why you're here—we need to talk about what happened yesterday with Yvette. But before we do that, I want you to know that I just received the monthly report from I.T. You know they monitor the website Patient Comments Count and you continue to be the highest ranked nurse in the hospital. Patients appreciate the attention you give them and they want to let others know that. Thank you for doing such a great job in that area.

Kim is using an important technique known as "contrasting" with this comment. Her goal is to put Simon at ease, as well as to make it clear that the agenda is limited to the incident and not about anything else. For many of us, a call for a private meeting from a supervisor ignites fear that we have done "something wrong." Even if we can't think of what that might be, we begin going over our behavior and wonder what has been reported to the boss. We may enter the meeting feeling defensive and uneasy. Then, Kim gets straight to the point:

As I mentioned earlier, Simon, we need to discuss what happened between you and Yvette, so I want to hear your perspective on the situation. Clearly, there are some issues between you two that are spilling over and beginning to have a negative impact on our work environment and on others. Our hospital needs to be a sanctuary for our patients—where they can get better without unnecessary distractions. My meeting with you is the first step in understanding and resolving what seems to be ongoing tension on the floor. This can't continue; it's not productive. But I am optimistic that the three of us can come up with a solution together if we approach it the right way.

Kim then describes what the process will be to give Simon important information about what to expect:

I will also be meeting with Yvette to hear her perspective. After that, a half hour before the shift change meeting today, I would like the three of us to meet to discuss ways to work more collaboratively so that patients get the best care possible, we have a positive work environment, and you and Yvette have a respectful working relationship with each other. Are you on board with that, Simon?

Simon nods and Kim continues:

I won't repeat your private information to Yvette but I will bring up general issues that need to be resolved. I will be taking notes for my records and may discuss this issue privately with our Employee Relations representative, if I feel it is necessary. They have strict guidelines about confidentiality so rest assured your private information will be kept confidential. As you know, the issue of arguing in front of patients is against hospital policy so we will need to look at that as well as any other policy issue or standards of care concerns that may arise. To be clear, this is not a disciplinary session. Apparently, you both were upset. My goal is to talk through the issues and see what we can do to resolve the situation together. Can you tell me what happened?

With the stage set, Simon now has an opportunity to present his view of the situation:

I am still so upset about it. I want you to know that I didn't argue back with Yvette; she just attacked me. I was in the break room, on my break. Louie, the ward clerk, had given me a couple of cards that were addressed to me. So, I had just read the bad news that Mr. Newman had passed away; his wife wrote to thank me for his care. It was sad; he was such a good man. Kim, I was minding my own business, during my break, reading the card. That was when Yvette came in and started yelling at me about it and criticizing me for caring about people. As I was leaving, she yelled at me in the hall. I was so embarrassed.

Simon provides some information that was not available before: the context of the conflict and what kind of emotional state he was in. Before he says much more, Kim makes sure that he knows she is listening carefully and that she really understands the situation from his perspective:

So, it seems from what you are telling me that you were trying to take care of reading and reacting to the news privately. Let me know a bit more about your working relationship with Yvette.

Simon suddenly decides to withdraw from the conversation by proposing a one-sided solution to the situation:

I should just try harder to get along with her. I could open cards at home so if I react to any news, it won't bother her. I think that will solve the problem.

It would be very tempting for a manager to accept that quick fix and move on to the other aspects of the job. But Kim wants to ensure that the situation is not repeated and that they achieve a more lasting resolution. She points out the danger of his suggestion. It won't just go away!

Simon, if the situation were that simple, it wouldn't have gotten to this point. I want us to work through these issues. Tell me some more about what it has been like for you lately, working with Yvette.

And so he starts again, albeit reluctantly:

Not so good. She is definitely one of the best nurses on the floor with the technical aspects of the job, but . . . I don't know . . . .

And again, Kim encourages him to talk by reinforcing her interests in having this conversation:

I know this is hard, Simon, but the purpose of this meeting, as I mentioned before, is for me to get as much understanding as possible about your point of view so that we can work through these issues and go back to focusing on our mission—"quality patient care for the whole person."

This is the encouragement he needs:

That's just it, exactly. Yvette thinks just because she is technically good, she is providing quality patient care but she forgets the part about the WHOLE person. I really believe in caring for the whole person; that is why I get close to patients. I see them as people first and I want to provide the kind of attention I would want if I were in their shoes. Her bedside care just doesn't match her administrative nursing skills. You know how we are supposed to make sure to see each of our patients two times each shift? Yvette certainly goes into the room, but all she does is check the monitors and IV lines. She doesn't even talk to the patients. She may see herself as efficient, but I don't think that's the goal. Simply going in the room and ignoring the human being who's in there just isn't right.

Without taking his side, Kim again makes sure Simon knows that she is listening:

A couple of issues that are important to you have to do with that balance of the technical and administrative skills required of an RN with the bedside nursing skills that humanize the hospital experience for people and help them feel cared for. Clearly we will need to discuss the standards of care in both areas.

And Simon takes another shot at his colleague:

You make it sound so reasonable, Kim. I know both are important but I am just not sure that Yvette does. She is just so critical of everything I do. I just don't get it.

Kim now deflects the criticism back to the issue after acknowledging his unstated feelings:

So it seems like you're feeling judged by Yvette for your style of nursing, Simon. Mrs. Cruz, the woman who complained about the incident, had high praise for your style, but was rightfully upset that she had to hear the arguing. I was able to talk to her and let her know that this would be handled appropriately.

Simon, true to his "conflict-avoidance approach" to life, demonstrates his desire to fix the situation with Alma Cruz, the patient:

I am so sorry that she had to hear all that. Here she is, recovering from surgery. She is a nice lady, former teacher, you know. I would just hate to have her leave with a bad impression of us. I think I will apologize to her. Don't worry; I won't say anything negative about Yvette.

Kim offers encouragement:

Simon, thank you for offering to apologize to Mrs. Cruz. I think that would be a nice gesture. She even said that her daughter was

going to help her post something about you on the Patient Comments
Count website. She wants everyone to know about you, and her
daughter said that was the best way.

And now, Simon finally reveals a personal grievance and a concern:

I like to print out the comments from the website to inspire us on
the floor. We get a lot of nice cards too. The thing is Yvette doesn't
appreciate that at all. Some other nurses have been complaining
about how often Yvette calls and texts in the break room, which is
more often than just when she has a break. I tell them it's none of
our business. I just worry about the patients, you know, because of
all of the monitors. I thought the policy was that no cell phones could
be used within three feet of the monitors, right? Well, it seems to
me that Room 204 is less than three feet from the wall of the break
room, you know?

Kim senses that it's time to conclude the conversation *before* the key
issue is lost. She acknowledges what Simon has said, and she uses her
authority to give him instructions about her expectations for the next
meeting:

You are proud of the comments on the website and you like to share
them with others. There also seems to be a concern about the cell
phone use in the break room. This is helpful feedback for me, Simon.
Thank you for speaking openly. I would like you to think about what
you could do to improve the situation with Yvette because when we
meet before the shift change today, we will be discussing the situa-
tion and working on improving the relationship between you two.
My interests are to have good teamwork on the floor, to follow our
mission, and to have all nurses conduct themselves in a professional
manner. Please also consider how Yvette might see the situation, so
that you will be better prepared to come up with options that meet
everyone's interests. See you at 2:30.

Simon makes one last attempt to avoid talking directly to Yvette:

I have an idea. Why don't we each just write down our suggestions
and give them to you? I have a couple of patients being admitted

today and that just takes so much time. I could write down my ideas tonight. Then we won't have to bother Yvette this way. . . .

Kim realizes that this conflict-avoidant employee who is reluctant to participate needs additional encouragement to participate in the process:

Simon, I realize that you are busy, but this is a priority and a face-to-face discussion is in order. I can request that the evening nurse comes in a half hour early. Would that help?

Simon's responds:

Oh, I wouldn't want to bother her.

Kim tries to reach him by asking a "reality-testing question," which will help Simon truly think through his avoidance of managing this issue with Yvette:

What do you think is going to happen if we don't work through these issues, Simon? I assure you that I will make it a safe conversation.

By asking a question to make him think, she finally gets a commitment from Simon to be part of a joint meeting:

I don't think I can take her criticism. But I guess it won't stop if we don't all talk it out. Thank you for helping me with this, Kim. I will think about it and see you at 2:30.

KIM BROWN'S PRIVATE MEETING WITH RN YVETTE JONES

Then, Kim Brown meets with RN Yvette Jones. The meeting begins with the same information about what to expect, assurances about confidentiality within the limits of hospital policy, and a comment about how other members of the department are affected. She ends with the same invitation to Yvette to talk about her perspective.

As happened with Simon, Yvette's first response is to apologize before launching into a pent-up explanation for her behavior:

First off, let me apologize for the incident with Simon; I take full responsibility for that patient complaint. You will never hear about me yelling at him in public again. But I just have had it with his emotional meltdowns on the job. This is not the first time I have found him upset in the break room. He shouldn't be working with the elderly if he can't handle the fact that our patients often die. He has no sense of appropriate professional boundaries.

After assuring Yvette that she has been listening and repeating her promise of confidentiality, as well as acknowledging that she has already met with Simon, Kim goes a little deeper:

What other concerns do you have about your working relationship with Simon that are possibly a problem for you on the job?

Yvette has some interesting new information:

Well, a couple of things, actually. I have had a few patients complain to me about how many tries it takes Simon to start an IV. One patient asked me if that nice man is really a nurse or if he was some kind of pastor. She asked, "Is he supposed to be able to do that?" I assured her that it wasn't outside of his responsibilities as a nurse to start an IV. The other thing is that Simon still doesn't get the EMR (Electronic Medical Records System). I know there have been some glitches, but he SHOULD do a better job documenting. The last thing is just simply annoying, but since you asked, it has to do with the nurse's station. Simon seems to think of it as his own personal shrine. Have you noticed all of the cards and photos he has there? He even prints things from the computer, e-mails and such from that website, for goodness sake.

Kim demonstrates that she has been listening, as she did with Simon, by paraphrasing the key issues and then she turns to an issue that Simon raised:

Another issue that has come to my attention is your cell phone use in the break room. Can you tell me about that?

Yvette has a reaction:

Oh, that, well I have just had some personal issues that I am dealing with lately. . . . I am not sure what that has to do with Simon.

It is then that Kim realizes that she just made an error in judgment. This was not the right time to raise that issue. Yvette is right; it has nothing to do with Simon. Internally, Kim panics a bit, but as a seasoned manager she doesn't let that show. She also doesn't want to let Yvette know that the information came from Simon. Thoughtfully, Kim responds:

> You are right; it doesn't have anything to do with Simon. But, since we are here and we are discussing workplace issues, this is something that I want to talk to you about. I have two concerns: one is the number of personal calls you are making and texts you are sending. You can certainly use your phone during your breaks, but if it's more than that, it's a problem since it takes you away from patient care and your other responsibilities. The other issue is that the break room is close to patient rooms where there are monitors. The policy of no cell phones within three feet of a patient's room is very troubling, honestly. It is such a difficult policy to enforce with the families of the patients. I am thinking about talking to HR about modifying this policy. But meanwhile, it needs to be followed.

Then Kim notices Yvette's "nonverbal behavior"—she has started to look down and her normally confident appearance seems to change.

> You have become very quiet, Yvette. Is everything okay?

Yvette seems almost eager to unburden herself:

> Oh, I don't like to bring personal matters to work, but Manuel, my husband, lost his job and, you know, it's pretty tough on him and on me. We might lose the house, so I have been texting and calling to see about refinancing and trying to get us some debt counseling, and it just takes some effort. . . .

Kim realizes that this is personal information that she will need to retain confidentially. She also knows that she is not a counselor. She reassures Yvette, makes the appropriate referral, and concludes the session.

> I am very sorry to hear that, Yvette. You know that we have a good employee assistance program for employees and their families. You

might want to talk to them. I will keep the reasons for your phone calls confidential, but you need to know that the issue of the three-foot rule is very important. I am going to talk to HR today about this policy and may have an answer by this afternoon when we meet. Please also do your best to make the calls during your break; if that is just not possible, come and see me. I will see you at 2:30 today with Simon. Between now and then, please think about how this situation has perhaps impacted him and think about what you can offer to improve things between you. That will really help to facilitate our discussion. Thank you, Yvette.

With that, Stage One of The Exchange is complete.

WHY HOLD SEPARATE MEETINGS?

In addition to the organizational personnel reasons for separate meetings there are practical reasons to hold separate meetings. Occasionally a manager will just want to get the employees together and "hash out" the problem. While that may work, we have found that people need a little time to prepare for such an encounter; otherwise it might degenerate into a tense encounter or perhaps conclude with a solution that is not satisfactory to anyone, even if it provides a temporary ending to one situation. Without The Exchange, the Nursing Department is likely to wind up with one or both of the nurses involved feeling undervalued and in the long term one or both might leave. Certainly the coworkers on the floor would likely take sides as to who was "right" and who was "wrong," and the conflict would continue. In contrast, The Exchange usually ends in a comprehensive, workable agreement and an improved climate in the workplace. Each stage is important to achieving such a resolution. Stage One is critical for several reasons:

> ▸ *Saving face for the parties.* One of the key elements to successful conflict resolution is "face saving." The concept of *face saving,* or how one sees oneself, seems to be a value in every culture. In the United States, a very individualistic culture, it essentially means not being in a position to be embarrassed

or humiliated by another person. A private meeting allows an individual to explain what happened without having to defend one's actions. When there are witnesses, studies of conflict resolution show, most human beings tend to become defensive or feel they have to justify their actions by escalating the seriousness of what happened.

▶ *Gathering important data.* In the beginning of The Exchange, one goal is simply for the manager or facilitator to gather information. He or she will need two kinds of information:

  • First are the facts about *verifiable behaviors.* These represent the "what" of a dispute.

  • The second type of information allows the facilitator to discover the *interests* of each party. This type of information is often unstated but crucial data about the impact of the situation on the individuals involved. Interests are the underlying "why" of a conflict—the motivations, expectations, fears, hopes, or concerns that led to the actions involved in the situation.

Knowing both the "what" and the "why" of the situation is fundamental to a comprehensive and satisfying resolution.

▶ *Providing an opportunity for each party to vent.* The private meeting is a chance for each employee to vent a little, without risking permanent damage. Vulnerability is often associated with expression of feelings. In American culture most people like to be thought of as strong and any public expression of weakness is to be avoided. Stage One allows people to express their feelings, without becoming too exposed to the person with whom they are in conflict. Once expressed, those feelings are not as likely to erupt into angry and hurtful words when the parties do come together—words that might sabotage all the good work hoped for in the joint discussion.

▶ *Providing information to the parties about The Exchange.*
In order for individuals to do their best they need as much
information as possible about what is expected.
- They need to know the purpose of the meeting and the
process.
- They need to know about confidentiality—what records will
be kept?
- They need to know the steps of the process and what is next.

This is information for the manager to provide, and it will
set a climate in which people can safely discuss important
issues.

Stage One is important but it is only a beginning. Next is Stage
Two, the private session a manager has alone or with a coach.

CHAPTER 4

The Exchange, Stage Two: Developing the Agenda

After her meeting with Yvette Jones, Kim Brown closed her door and took out her notes from the earlier conversation with Simon Peters. She realized that the next step would be very important. Both Simon and Yvette were good nurses and both had added depth to her department. But their personal conflict reflected deeper concerns than just a clash of styles or personalities. She knew that Dr. Phillips and his patient, Mrs. Alma Cruz, were not the only ones aware of the situation. Kim also knew that there would soon be rumors about who did what and why it mattered. And she knew that her own reputation as a nursing manager was involved.

She thought for a moment and then dialed Drew Johnson, the head of Employee Relations.

> *Okay, Drew. I've met with both my nurses and now I'd like to take you up on your offer to work with me on this situation. I've scheduled a meeting with both of them for 2:30 this afternoon, so if you are available, I'd like to go over my thoughts about how to conduct the joint meeting.*

Drew responded:

> *Glad to. I'll come over in about 20 minutes. I just have to finish up a report for Radha. I'm really glad you called.*

STAGE TWO IN GREATER DETAIL

Stage Two of The Exchange is vital to the success of the process. It is the opportunity for the facilitator to reflect on what has been said by each individual and to devise an agenda based on conflict-resolution strategies that encompass both the joint conversation of Stage Three and the problem-solving process that occurs in Stage Four. Some of the things that need to be considered are:

▶ *The role of the manager.* Kim is obviously a stakeholder in this conflict; that is, she is not only affected by the conflict but she has a clear interest in its satisfactory resolution. So she is not neutral. The conflict has to be resolved and she is the one responsible for that resolution. But her success, the department's success, and ultimately the employees' success depends on their participation in the problem-solving process.

A key principle of conflict resolution is that when people participate in the process, they will have a stake in the outcome. Involving Simon and Yvette constructively will be important. Part of Kim's job will be to convince them not only that she is sincere but also that she has not made a personal judgment about who is to blame—who is "right" and who is "wrong."

Managers should and do clarify hospital policy, procedures, and acceptable workplace behavior to employees on an ongoing basis; there *is* a "right" and "wrong," in this regard. This is to be distinguished from judging employees' *personal* reactions and feelings, which have no right or wrong. All of us react negatively to someone who says, "You shouldn't feel that way."

Kim will need to think carefully about how the discussion topics are framed. As much as possible, she needs to be able to think about a neutral way to frame the issues to help engage her employees in the best way possible. She will also need to monitor their communication with each other and help them speak in ways that will be helpful and not hurtful.

▶ *The language.* Words are important. As the saying goes, *"sticks and stones may break my bones, but words will never hurt me."* We are not so sure that words don't have a longer-lasting impact on people. Words, tone, and body language do matter. In stressful encounters, people will always remember the tone in which other people have spoken, even though they tend to remember only a certain percentage of the actual words they hear. Therefore, finding the *right* words and considering carefully the tone make everything easier. So Kim will clearly be looking to frame the topics for discussion in language that is not inflammatory and avoids giving the impression to either employee that the process is unfair.

▶ *The order of addressing the issues of the conflict.* Kim has already demonstrated to both Simon and Yvette that she understood their points of view. Now she will need to help them understand each other. A general strategy for doing this is to include both emotional and factual topics in the discussion. We refer to the former as *impact* and to the latter as *issues.* Both provide data that need to be exchanged in the course of resolving the situation.

▶ *The icebreaker.* A beginning topic or icebreaker will provide new information and set the tone. The idea is that people often need a nonconfrontational way to begin a difficult discussion. Both Simon and Yvette are likely to be nervous and defensive at the thought of talking to each other. Remember in the last chapter how they both gave reasons *not* to have to meet? Kim will be looking for a subject that will put them both at ease and perhaps even distract them, for a moment, so that they can approach the difficult subjects more thoughtfully.

In many settings, the Employee Relations staff help to implement The Exchange process by encouraging managers and supervisors to utilize it in appropriate settings. They tend to champion the cause of effective conflict resolution because they often see the negative results of ineffective attempts at resolving conflict, or of managers choosing to ignore it completely.

Let's listen in on the discussion as Drew Johnson, St. Sonia's head of Employee Relations, helps Kim prepare for the joint meeting with the nurses, Simon and Yvette. Drew and Kim are seated together at a round table. Kim has a notebook and looks at it occasionally as she is pointing out different things from her previous meetings with Simon and Yvette. She takes brief notes as they talk:

Thanks so much for meeting with me, Drew. This conversation will really help me figure out what I should use for the agenda. I feel like I am really getting The Exchange process better now. Stage One went very well with each employee. But since this is new for me I really appreciate you taking some time coaching me through it.

His response was what she had hoped for:

Kim, I am pleased that you are embracing the new Exchange program we are implementing. And, I want to be a resource for you. That's one thing Employee Relations is for! Remember, I will be documenting this conversation for our records but, as you probably know, this new Exchange process is being handled separately from our disciplinary system, so it won't be documented in anyone's official personnel record. No one has access to this information except Employee Relations staff members. My role here is to help you gain confidence in using the process so that conflicts are resolved efficiently and effectively at the manager level. Tell me how it went.

So Kim begins:

As you know, Yvette and Simon argued on the floor, in front of a patient. They have a major difference in styles that is disrupting their ability to work collaboratively and in a respectful manner. Of course, other nurses in the department are starting to feel the tension. I can't let this escalate any further. It's a very negative situation, particularly for a hospital! Simon is a real sweetie, a very good-hearted man.

Drew has a comment:

Yes, I remember you saying that about him earlier. Patients often mention him in the online survey—"great nurse! We loved him."

Kim responds:

You got it. They love him. He uses the standard of care regarding two interactions with each patient every shift as an opportunity to interact positively with patients and their families. On the other hand, Yvette doesn't do the bedside nursing as well, and she really doesn't seem to understand why it is so important. But I don't want you to think she isn't a good nurse; she is very professional and very competent. We all rely on her to help us out with new technology and data entry. She's just not a warm and fuzzy person. We definitely have to discuss these work style and attitude differences.

Drew nods and continues:

Excellent, Kim. You are on the right track. Keep going. What else do you think needs to be addressed when you all meet?

Kim responds:

Well, Yvette feels that Simon doesn't set personal boundaries. That is very challenging for some nurses in gerontology, and honestly, there is not a clear policy around it. We do deal with people close to the end of their lives, you know. Some go into hospice or pass away soon after we see them, and good nurses have to be personally prepared so that they can prepare the patients and their families for whatever outcome seems realistic.

Drew is sympathetic:

I know; that is challenging. You should be ready to voice your expectations around professional standards of conduct in the meeting. Since it not only affects them but all of our nurses here at the hospital. Why don't I work with you and the other supervisors over the next month to define a standard policy? Let's talk about that possibility sometime soon. What other specific challenges do Simon and Yvette have when they work together?

Kim replies:

Yvette has worked here for five years, and no one has ever complained about her yelling at anyone before. She has some family stress right now that I am sure contributed to the incident. I just feel taking a hard-line disciplinary approach isn't the way to go. She did take responsibility for the mistake, and I appreciate that. She is sometimes perceived as being distant and insensitive with patients, so maybe we could deal with that?

Drew has a thought about how to frame this delicate topic so that it will not give Yvette the impression that Kim thinks she is a "bad nurse." Overall, Yvette's performance reviews were excellent in many categories and average in others, so it was important to Drew that Kim understands that this conversation is about Simon and Yvette's different styles of nursing and their working relationship, rather than about a disciplinary issue over any lack of competence as RNs.

What if you labeled one of the Issues on your agenda Patient Relations? This way you could focus on boundaries and the expectation of treating the whole person. That's also a great way to help Yvette and Simon relate their contributions to our hospital's mission statement.

With the topic framed in nonescalating language, Kim now has a chance to identify a possible opening or icebreaker topic that could actually help all three of them begin this conversation on a positive note.

Good, I like that.

Kim, after checking her notes, looks up at Drew, and states:

Yvette did complain about Simon's inability to find a vein, stating that he takes more than two times to do it. I have had a recent complaint about that from the spouse of a patient; he was a doctor so he was quite critical of a lot things. But, that is a different problem. For now, should I bring up the competency issue, you know, the technical skills?

Drew doesn't seem surprised:

This is a common problem, even for seasoned nurses. Don't we have an in-house seminar on working with obese and elderly patients?

Kim replies:

Yes, you are right, we do have that class. Both obese and elderly patients have veins that are tough to find. Should I just tell him to take the class?

Drew clarifies further:

This meeting isn't about an assessment regarding their skills, but to engage them in a conversation about their work styles and working relationship. Perhaps you could have them talk about their perceptions of the balance of the bedside nursing skills with the administrative nursing skills so they will understand the importance of each. The idea of a class may come up because everyone will be looking for solutions during the latter part of the meeting. We really want them to come up with some of the solutions AND it's good for you to have some ideas in mind as well.

Kim now has two subject matter issues: *patient relations* and *nursing style*. Since she is new to using The Exchange, you will see that she does fall into a discussion of technical skills (a performance issue), as she is accustomed to that type of conversation. You will also see that she will find a way to work through this error and use it to her advantage. For now, in her agenda, each topic (patient relations and nursing style) affects both nurses and is framed in neutral language. Kim continues:

Now, what about the EMR [electronic medical records] system? You know the doctors have commented on how well Yvette keeps records. She complained about Simon but really, he's not the only one in my unit that could use help. That system is not very intuitive. I could certainly compliment Yvette on that and see where it goes from there. Maybe we can build on her successes with that?

Continuing the conversation and getting Drew's feedback helps Kim develop a list of issues for the meeting. Drew suggests a conversation about Simon's and Yvette's future working relationship and how Kim might address that.

Kim responds:

Well, a core value of the hospital is teamwork. *Maybe I could bring that up to clarify my expectations about it and to help them find ways to work better as a team. Perhaps we could talk about what teamwork means. Yvette needs to understand this. This could also tie into Yvette's complaint about Simon's cards all around the nurses' station. Teamwork does include everyone using the station, right?*

Finding a common umbrella word like *teamwork* will take the sting out of some of the complaints Simon and Yvette have about each other and allow them to address this critical subject nondefensively. At the conclusion of the Issue discussion, Drew points out:

Perhaps those are enough issues for the meeting; it seems like you are hitting the big ones. What about the impact of the situation? You want to make sure that they both get to express the impact on them and you should be prepared to discuss the impact from your perspective on the work environment and staff effectiveness.

Drew is subtly reminding Kim that the joint meeting needs to be focused on two or three *issues* that can be effectively addressed in a half hour. If the discussion goes on too long, people become mentally exhausted and the good energy that was present in the beginning starts to dissipate. But he does want to make sure that the key second type of concern, the *impact*, will not be ignored. They will need to talk about how each of them was personally affected by the situation.

Kim replies:

Well, they will need to report how they have been feeling at work lately. I better watch myself with that word feeling. *Yvette might react to that. How should I say it? Oh, yes, I'll just ask them each to say how the situation has impacted them.*

Drew continues:

Great. Now what about the icebreaker?

Kim replies:

Maybe I can ask them how (or why) they got into nursing. I know this is Simon's second career, so maybe there's something to that.

While Kim already has one possible icebreaker in mind—their mission at the hospital—she is now refining her question to make it more likely that each nurse will have an opportunity to pass on information that the other would have no knowledge of—the original motivation for entering the field of health care. The best icebreakers are personal and inspirational. They need to invite answers that cannot be disputed, and they should provide an opportunity for the speaker to say something positive about him- or herself. This is important because most people feel badly about being identified as a party to a conflict; some even feel like failures. Here is an opportunity to allow them to be reminded of their early motivations and goals.

Drew concludes his discussion with Kim:

Very nice work, Kim. This should get easier every time you use it. Now, let's review what you wrote down. Next time I would recommend that you do it on your own. Keep me in the loop, though. I want to know how the process is working for you.

Drew and Kim review the agenda given in Table 4.1 carefully. Based on their conversation, Kim has noted the *issues* she wants to address, the questions she wants to ask about *impact*, and the *introductory* icebreaker topic.

As you gain more familiarity with The Exchange, you will no doubt find yourself listening in different ways as you conduct the Stage One private meetings. You will begin to find common issues that affect people in a healthcare setting and you will also find that these are common human issues.

Listen for situations in which:

▶ One person feels disrespected by the other.

▶ One person feels treated unfairly.

▶ The participants feel that their own ability to work effectively is being threatened by the conflict.

TABLE 4.1 | STAGE TWO AGENDA

ICEBREAKER	What made you decide to go into healthcare, and, specifically, senior care?
IMPACT	How has it been working together lately? It seems like you don't feel like you are being treated respectfully.
ISSUES	Patient relations
	Nursing style
	Professional boundaries
	Treating "the whole person"
	Teamwork

You will begin to realize in Stage Two that most conflicts escalate beyond mere disagreements when there is something else involved. That something is the *impact* or emotions the participants experience. Unless people can recognize and express this impact, and unless they can understand that the other person has *also* been affected, any resolution will likely be superficial because the underlying issues will not have been addressed. The predictable result is that the conflict will resurface and cause more frustration and undermine the good intentions of those who tried to resolve it.

CHAPTER 5

The Exchange, Stage Three: The Joint Meeting

S tage Three is what makes The Exchange different from other forms of conflict resolution. It is the heart of The Exchange process. If Stage Three is conducted well, it gives the participants an opportunity to deal with the issues in conflict in a holistic way, not just superficially by declaring a truce, but by truly getting to the bottom of what caused the problem in the first place so it won't resurface again under different circumstances. Stage Three is also an opportunity for the parties to practice a new, open, and respectful way to communicate with each other.

Having the plan developed in Stage Two, based on the private meetings with each of the parties, is a crucial tool to:

▸ Help a facilitator keep the conversation focused.

▸ Make efficient progress through all the issues.

▸ Achieve productive problem solving.

Without an agenda it would be easy for the meeting to become sidetracked and dominated by the complaining and misunderstanding that caused the original conflict in the first place.

STAGE THREE IN GREATER DETAIL

The goal of Stage Three is to build a foundation of at least minimum trust among all the participants and create an opportunity for constructive communication so that wise decisions will be made in Stage Four. To do this, the participants need to see each other as human beings rather than as enemies. One of the first topics for discussion, the *icebreaker*, is designed to serve this purpose. Only when the parties can talk civilly can they open up about how their lives and work have been affected by the conflict.

Before introducing the icebreaker, the manager must first lay the groundwork with an *opening statement*. If Kim Brown, the manager in our example, opens the conversation with the *icebreaker* ("What made you want to get into the nursing field?") with nothing said beforehand, the employees will react in a negative way, because the question seems to be out of place, given the fact that the stated purpose of the meeting is to find solutions to the specific issues confronting the employees. The manager needs to take the time to set the tone and reinforce the purpose of the meeting, and in some cases, even set forth the ground rules for the dialogue. It is not unlike any meeting that a manager initiates; the responsibility is on the manager to set forth the meeting parameters at the beginning. In this way, the employees get a sense of the greater context of the meeting, rather than being asked to dive into the agenda immediately. Sometimes, after setting forth the meeting goals, the manager will clarify the topics to be discussed in the meeting in *summary form* to let the employees know that their issues will be addressed.

After that initial opening statement, the manager poses the icebreaker to the employees. This very short conversation, in which the employees and the manager all participate, is to help find some common ground among them. It can improve the tone of the conversation to follow because this relaxed, positive discussion slightly changes the view that the employees have of one another.

One day, Drew Thompson, the head of Employee Relations, got a call from a director at the hospital. Drew recalled that the director's boss, a vice president (VP), had been an early advocate of The Exchange methodology and learned how to use it. The day after the VP finished learning the process, he returned to a brewing conflict between two high-level directors. The VP was able to facilitate an Exchange process, and the conflict was resolved. That director contacted Drew immediately, stating:

He [the VP] *had me with the icebreaker. Our private meeting (Stage One) was important to me because I got to tell him my perspective but I still expected he would simply fix everything for us. When he had us do the icebreaker at the beginning of the joint meeting, it put the conflict I had been having with the other director in context with the greater good that we had in common. We both were passionate about patient safety and I had been so fixated on the other director's different style and the way he talked to me, I forgot that. Once we did the icebreaker, everything changed for me. Sure, we had to work out the details, but I found myself motivated to figure it out* with *him. I have to learn this stuff.*

After the icebreaker sets the tone, it needs to be followed by the *impact question* and discussion—again, an intensely subjective one. Each participant needs to show the others the toll the situation has taken on him or her. If this doesn't happen, the unspoken feelings will not dissipate but will return to sabotage whatever useful agreement is made. There is a certain balance in workplace situations in which a manager wants the employees to share their reactions to the situation and how it has *affected them at work*, without exposing their *personal lives*.

It is worth taking the care to ask the impact question in a way that avoids going too deeply into the person's emotional space. For example, instead of saying, *"You seem to feel hurt and belittled by . . ."* the manager could say, *"It appears that both of you have been frustrated with the situation,"* or *"You seem like you don't believe you are being treated with respect."* Better yet, simply ask, *"How has it been working together lately?"*

The *impact* question is used to allow each employee to hear and learn that the conflict has affected not just him or her but also has affected the other person and, perhaps, the department as well. It is important to make sure that the conversation stays somewhat controlled during this exchange so what is said does not lead to an attack. Again, not much time will be spent on the impact question. The purpose here is simply to acknowledge that the reactions, concerns, and feelings do exist; it certainly is not to try to fix them.

Once the two first topics, the *icebreaker* and the *impact* question, have been discussed by the participants and their answers acknowledged by the facilitator, the participants are directed to discuss the specific issues, one at a time. The manager's job with the *issue discussion* is to:

▸ Make sure that there is a clear understanding of each person's perspective.

▸ Clarify the perspective of the department or the manager.

▸ Move, eventually, from the issue discussion to problem solving.

The key is for the manager to lead the participants in a *positive* verbal exchange of understanding, on both an emotional and a factual level, of how each participant is experiencing the situation.

KIM BROWN'S JOINT MEETING WITH RN SIMON PETERS AND RN YVETTE JONES

Let's take a look at how Kim Brown, Head Nurse Geriatrics, handles the joint meetings with the two St. Sonia's nurses. Promptly at 2:30 p.m. that day Kim sits down with her two employees, RN Simon Peters and RN Yvette Jones. They take their places at an oval table in one of the hospital's private conference rooms. Cell phones have been turned off and to anyone passing by, the scene looks like a normal consultation.

Kim opens the conversation:

Busy day, wasn't it? I appreciate that you two managed to get everything done so you could come to meet with me. Well, we have about a half hour to talk through the issues. The goal in this meeting is for us to come to a better understanding of each of your interests and the needs we have for teamwork *and* quality patient care *here at the hospital. This is a confidential meeting among the three of us. I will keep a record of what we decide on for my own file. I will send an e-mail to each of you to confirm what our decisions are today and I will follow up with you both. My expectations for this meeting are that we will work hard to resolve the lingering issues between you and that we will show respect to each other during this discussion. Is that acceptable to both of you?*

Kim then gives a brief overview of her agenda. Note that she does not share *every* detail of her notes. What the employees need is a *general idea* of what is to come so that they can participate successfully. Too much detail serves only to confuse and even cause anxiety that this meeting could take a very long time and be very difficult. So it is important to be clear that this is not a "life list" of grievances; it is just an opportunity to deal with a recent incident.

Kim begins:

> *So we will be talking about patient relations, both around professional boundaries and treating the* whole person, *as stated in our mission. We will talk about your different styles of nursing, and we will address the teamwork expected from nurses who work together. If we talk about these issues, will that address the major items that you both have been dealing with while working together on the job lately?*

The list of issues is short. They are dealing with *one* incident and its roots and consequences, not years of documented behavioral problems. The Exchange process is *not* about discipline; it is about solving a problem.

Although Simon agrees with what Kim has asked, Yvette is not so accommodating:

> *I don't get it. Is this some kind of group disciplinary session? I already apologized for the incident, Kim, and . . .*

Without directly responding to Yvette's comment, yet acknowledging the progress already made in the private sessions, Kim moves back to the agenda for the afternoon:

> *I want to acknowledge that you have taken responsibility for the incident, Yvette. Frankly, I see that incident as the tip of the iceberg; what it tells me is that we need to work to develop a better working relationship between the two of you if we are going to achieve the standards of care required of us. So, to answer your question, Yvette, no, this is not a disciplinary session. As I mentioned to you before, this is an opportunity to talk through the issues and the differences*

between you, to find common ground, and create new options for how you can work together successfully. Both of you, our patients, and the rest of the staff deserve this.

Now Kim makes clear her own interests in this situation. As their manager, she is a stakeholder as well as the facilitator of the discussion:

And as your supervisor, I need to have harmony on the floor and make sure we are focused on the right things.

Both nurses are, no doubt, a little nervous and also anxious to get to the real discussion, but Kim throws them slightly off balance with her suggestion:

Since there has been some tension, I would like to begin the discussion with a topic you are experts on; it's an icebreaker *to get the conversation started and will remind us all about what this work means to us. I am curious about what motivated each of you to get into nursing. Simon, I know this is your second career. Tell us about that change.*

Kim's choice of the *icebreaker* topic is one she believes would be easy for each of them to address and one on which she too has something to offer. She chose Simon to begin because she knew that he would be most likely to set a positive tone for what would follow and she wanted Yvette to have a model that was not negative—not another complaint. This is an opportunity for each nurse to look good to the other and to feel good about themselves. Often when employees feel summoned to a meeting, they enter the discussion with their defenses up. They are ready to defend themselves or criticize the other person. They are worried about being blamed. They are not quite ready to talk to each other!
Simon leaps at the chance to talk:

Well, I was an accountant for 10 years and people always told me that I didn't act like an accountant, whatever that means. I have to say it wasn't very fulfilling but I had always done well in math so it seemed to make sense when I was 20 years old and in college. Then my dad got real sick and had to go to hospice. Between all of the hospital visits and then hospice, I was overcome with the immediacy of a nurse's care—the combination of healing and the nurse's touch. I lost my father but I gained a new passion and I try to live that passion every day in honor of my dad.

Kim acknowledges what Simon shared:

I am sorry for the loss of your father. It seems like that situation profoundly affected your life.

It's amazing how powerful such an *acknowledgment* can be. Simon has probably never spoken about this before in front of a colleague, but it was his choice to go as deep as he did. There was no pressure from the manager to speak so personally.

Thanks, Kim. But, you know, he was almost 80 years old. He had a great life.

Kim now turns to Yvette for her turn at the icebreaker:

What about you, Yvette? How did you get into nursing?

Of course, Yvette has her own story to share:

Well, a couple of things. My mom died in a car wreck when I was 12 and I had three younger siblings. I just kind of took care of them. Plus, my grandpa was blind and I was often asked to help him out. So, the caretaker role came early. I didn't mind. I just did what I had to do. On the bright side, caring for my grandpa got me interested in senior care because I think the complexity of an aging body and different illnesses is a challenge and I want to provide competent nursing care for them.

Kim too has her own inspiration to relate and it is relevant to the conversation. Managers often find that sharing their own response to this question humanizes the conversation in a positive way:

It seems that both of you, actually all three of us, were affected by family events. Between a father who was a pharmacist, and a mother who was a licensed practical nurse, I was destined to enter this field. Fortunately, I really enjoy it.

To transition from the icebreaker to the impact question, Kim now points out the common threads of each story and gently raises the issue of different work styles that was so important in this conflict:

One thing I noticed as each of you spoke, in addition to the family connection, is that there is a passion and a drive to provide quality patient care. Though you talked about it in different ways, it is clearly there. Looking at the present situation, this tension in the workplace also has probably impacted each of you. Yvette, can you talk about how this situation with Simon has been building up for you?

Recognize that Kim alternates between choosing Simon and Yvette to talk first about the topics. This is a way to keep the process fair and balanced. It's surprising how often an employee notices who gets to start a discussion and then begins to draw conclusions about who is the "favorite."

Yvette takes the bait, runs with it, and launches into an attack about her colleague Simon:

I just think Simon needs to be more aware of professional boundaries. He wants to be best friends with all the patients and their families that come on this floor. Mr. Personality is a walking stereotype of some archaic version of nursing. He goes around . . .

Kim wants to hear about Yvette's own reaction first, not her complaints. The order of topics is important because Yvette and Simon need to have the opportunity to express their reactions to the situation before moving on. Otherwise, the impact of Yvette's own performance on others will not be addressed and will continue to haunt the nursing department. So Kim respectfully, but firmly, brings the conversation back to the original question.

Yvette was not trying to be difficult. She was doing what comes naturally to most of us—blame someone else or distract from any real internal examination of oneself by talking about the other person. Kim interrupts Yvette and continues:

Excuse me, Yvette; my question could have been clearer. We will definitely get to the details of each of the issues soon but, right now, just focus on what your reaction *to these issues has been. How has it been for you, Yvette? Before you answer that, Simon, I am going to ask you to* listen carefully *so that you will be able to repeat back the essence of what you understand about what Yvette has to say. You will get an opportunity, Simon, to describe the situation from your perspective as well in this meeting.*

This is something Simon needs to hear. He is not the only one affected.

Yvette continues:

Well, it just drives me nuts. I just get so frustrated with having to work with someone who needs to focus on the technical skills but doesn't seem to have the ability to do things right.

Kim knows that this point is critical to Yvette; if the message is not heard, she will not be able to move forward in this conversation. So Kim asks Simon to paraphrase Yvette's comments, an important technique to assure that a speaker is being heard and responded to in a respectful way. It is difficult for Kim to request this without sounding like a teacher or a parent. However, the danger of not asking the employees to do this is that an essential point of understanding will be missed and the speaker may feel dismissed and irrelevant.

Here's what Kim says:

Simon, what did you hear? You don't have to agree. I just want to be sure that you heard what Yvette wanted you to hear. This is obviously important to her.

Simon gives it a try:

Yvette becomes frustrated by my style. She thinks I need to focus on my technical skills. I am so sorry, Yvette, that you see me as a stereotypical archaic nurse. My goal is to be a model nurse so what you are telling me is that I am not what I want to be.

Kim now makes sure that the message sent by Yvette was the one received by Simon:

Yvette, is that what you wanted Simon to hear?

Always honest, Yvette comments:

Well, I guess . . .

Now it's important for Simon to address the same topic of the personal impact of the conflict. Kim asks him:

Simon, what about you? How has this been for you?

Simon replies:

Um, well, gee, I don't know. Yvette is probably right; I do need to work on getting IVs started. It is just hard for me sometimes with some of our patients. I also get, I don't know, nervous, when I feel that someone is judging me. Like recently, when Dr. Knipchild's wife was here. He was watching everything I did, with such an exasperated look. I am sure he just wanted the best for her, you know. But that made me do things worse than usual.

And then Simon adds a very important point:

That is how I feel when you are rolling your eyes at me, Yvette. I feel so self-conscious and clumsy.

Now it's Yvette's turn to be gently put on the spot by Kim:

What did you hear Simon say about how this situation is affecting him?

Yvette complies in her usual direct manner:

Oh, yeah, well, he gets worried, upset, loses his confidence.

And again Kim checks with Simon:

Is that what you wanted Yvette to hear, Simon?

Being asked to repeat someone else's words can be very uncomfortable, and it takes skill to coach individuals to do it. But it is very powerful because it helps the message of understanding become real. Occasionally, parties are not able to paraphrase each other and then the manager does it for them. In either situation, the point is that each person's words need to be articulated to his or her satisfaction. The message sent must be the one received. Typically, the manager only asks participants to do this with one or two topics, and especially with the impact question, to ensure clear understanding. It is worth the time and effort to slow down the conversation at this point since it will help each speaker let go of the weight of his or her emotional burden once the speaker senses that the other person finally "gets it," in other words, that his or her words have finally been heard. Then the conversation about the issues can be more logical and less emotional, and more progress can be made.

Kim senses now that the time has come to move ahead to a discussion of the issues and to begin Stage Four, the problem-solving stage of The Exchange. Some readers may realize that both parties have more to say to each other about their feelings and reactions and while that may be true, it is important not to get stuck here. This is not a psychological counseling session. It is an opportunity to resolve a problem, so it is important to begin thinking about how to do that. There probably won't be a magic moment when the parties look at each other and become friends. A manager *can* expect coworkers to have a professional working relationship and this process can help them get there by providing a moment when they exchange understanding of one another. That is enough for now.

In The Exchange, Stages Three and Four flow into each other, particularly when the conversation comes around to a discussion of the issues. There is a fluidity between Stage Three (developing understanding) and Stage Four (problem solving). As Stage Three progresses, the manager:

▶ First, makes sure that each employee has had the opportunity to express his or her perspective on the issues.

▶ Next, identifies the interests of each employee and the expectations of the department.

▶ Then all three participants (the manager and coworkers) discuss ways to improve those issues, and they begin Stage Four, a problem-solving discussion.

While this might sound circular, a better metaphor for The Exchange is a spiral. There may be a repeat of subject matter but the flow is upward toward resolution. With that in mind, let's look at Stage Four.

CHAPTER 6

The Exchange, Stage Four: Problem Solving

As anyone involved in a conflict has experienced, it's easier to keep complaining and blaming others than actually to work on resolving the situation. Much of this is human nature. After all, you know the "rules" about complaining. You also know the situation from your perspective and you are probably fairly comfortable describing it. It's interesting that every time people retell an incident in which they believe they were wronged, their perception of it becomes more difficult to put aside. All the old emotions are re-experienced; it's as if the brain imprints them more deeply with each retelling. And for the most part, people get trapped in remembering how they were wronged in the past.

Focused discussion to resolve the situation, however, is new for most people. You don't know the "rules." There is no common "history" to fall back on. The Exchange resolution process may feel a little uncomfortable because it's going to involve change. Change, even good change, is stressful. This is why having someone there to direct the resolution process is so helpful. Without direction from a trained facilitator like Kim Brown, the conversation would tend to go around in circles of the past. The Exchange offers an opportunity to move into the future.

STAGE FOUR IN GREATER DETAIL

This stage of The Exchange process is called "Problem Solving." It is Stage Four, the final crucial stage. Without Stage Four, completing

Stages One, Two, and Three of the process may make people feel good about having had a chance to talk but then they may feel disappointed, or even cheated, that no decisions were made. As a result the next time conflicts occur, people might be less likely to agree to participate in an Exchange or be able to work through the issues more respectfully on their own. The ultimate goal of The Exchange is to find *practical* solutions to whatever the conflict issues are.

It is important to begin this problem-solving stage early in the joint meeting, but not until the foundation of understanding, the *impacts*, has been laid. People like to feel they are making progress and nothing feels more like progress than a decision to do something. Often, there is an almost palpable sense of relief in the room when the manager:

▶ Initiates the discussion of the *issues* in Stage Three.

▶ Allows each person to state his or her perspective.

▶ Asks that options for resolving the issues be put on the table.

The decision-making process is flexible. It is not a straight line, as you will find out yourself when leading The Exchange, moving back and forth between Stages Three and Four. With each issue in controversy, the goal is to *define*, *determine* (interests), *develop*, *decide*, and, later, *document*.

▶ *Define.* First, the leader makes sure that everyone has the same understanding about the issues or at least that everyone understands how the *other* participants understand the issues.

▶ *Determine.* Then, the leader identifies each of the participants' interests and states the interests of the organization and work environment that the leader represents.

▶ *Develop.* Then, together, everyone in the room explores possible solutions; that is, they develop the issues by identifying potential solutions that meet the interests of each person including the manager/leader. It's fine to look at solutions that might not work as they may contain a particle of something that *would* work.

▶   *Decide.* Then, the participants come to agreement by select-
ing the best possible solutions.

▶   *Document.* Finally, the decision is written down. Again there
are lots of choices: e-mail, a memo, or an agreement form.
Most managers find sending an e-mail conveys that it is an
informal process, yet there is still a clear record. The point
is, people forget; our memories are fallible—our brains tend
to revise experiences, and people end up with different but
honest memories of the same situation. A written agreement
reinforces the work that has gone into producing it.

The written documentation of the decision is the only thing that is
kept on file. Where the file is located will vary from institution to institution. At St. Sonia's Hospital, the agreements are kept in the managers'
files.

Kim Brown's Problem-Solving Discussion with RN Simon Peters and RN Yvette Jones

Let's look at how MSN Kim Brown, RN Simon Peters, and RN Yvette
Jones participated in the *issue* discussion of Stage Four of their conflict. When we left them, Kim had ensured that both Simon and Yvette
understood that the situation had a real impact on them both and on
others in the hospital as well.

Recognizing that you can't "fix" feelings but you can talk about
them, Kim wants to move to another item on her agenda, regarding
nursing style. But she decides to seize the opportunity to talk about
technical skills since Simon brought it up:

*Simon, you mentioned that you think that Yvette is right about your
technical skills, specifically, starting an IV. Please talk about that.*

Simon is a little sheepish:

Well, I know we have the two poke rule, *but sometimes, I have to
admit, it takes me three or four tries. I just keep thinking that I will
get better at it.*

Kim gives him credit, but she is clear that it is a practice that needs to be changed:

Thank you for acknowledging that. This is a serious issue that we need to address, Simon, because of our standard of care regarding IV competency.

Kim then moves into problem-solving mode with Simon:

What ideas do you have about improving that skill?

Naturally, Yvette has an idea for Simon:

They have the best classes in the training department, and I would highly recommend that you take one. They only last a couple of hours and you can do it on work time.

Kim needs to make sure that Simon is taking some responsibility—that it is his decision also, not just Yvette's.

Would you be willing to do that, Simon?

Simon responds:

Sure, okay, yes, I will look online after this meeting.

As his manager, Kim also takes some responsibility for the resolution to this problem:

Why don't you and I take a moment together at the end of this meeting and find a good class for you? After taking the class, how will we make sure that you feel more comfortable and confident in doing this part of your job, Simon?

Yvette tentatively makes an offer:

I could check his work.

Understanding the genuineness of the offer but knowing their history and the different styles of the two nurses, Kim recognizes that this could be a setup for future problems, so she heads it off:

That is really nice, Yvette, but I was thinking maybe Daniela could observe Simon a few times. She has a lot of training experience

here at the hospital. After we check about the course, what if we ask
Daniela if she would be willing to observe you do it a few times and
if you could go to her with questions. Would that be acceptable?

Simon nods; he is relieved that Yvette will not be observing him.
Kim adds to her agenda again, to balance the conversation: personal
cell phone use. This time Kim begins with her own acknowledgment of
being a part of the situation and its resolution:

I do want you both to know that I have spoken to HR about
modifying the cell phone policy. Beginning next week, at the first of
the month, we are officially going to allow cell phone calls only in the
family waiting room, which is 10 feet away from the closest patient
room. I will be making that announcement and posting signs after
this meeting. That means for you and the other staff members on the
floor, personal cell phone calls and texts will need to be made during
your breaks, off the floor. I know that is inconvenient, but we just
have to be careful with how the use of this equipment is perceived
by others.

Now, Kim moves on to another issue that affects teamwork on the
floor—the new electronic recordkeeping program (EMR).

Speaking of equipment, I want to acknowledge your expertise with
the EMR, Yvette. This new program has taken many of us, myself
included, some time to get accustomed to. By the way, I have had
many compliments about your thoroughness, Yvette.

Again, Yvette returns to her criticism about Simon's lack of professionalism. She blurts out when she sees Simon roll his eyes and wince at
the mention of electronic data:

Kim responds to Yvette and then questions Simon:

Thanks, Yvette . . . but, Simon, this is another area that you need to
work on. This is information that could save a patient's life! Why
can't you figure it out?

Simon reacts to Yvette and Kim, stung by what seems like an unfair
charge. Even though the employees are ready to problem solve, certain
triggers bring out emotions:

Wait a minute! I am insulted that you assume I can't figure it out. Yvette, I was an accountant for 10 years. All I did was stare at computers day after day. No one can say that I can't figure out how to put data in. I admit that I have a reaction to doing it. I walked away from a better-paying job because I wanted to get away from that. Part of my reaction is just not wanting to do it and part of it is being completely upset about how much time you sit there staring at the computer instead of interacting with the patients! [Simon pauses to gain control of himself.] *I am sorry. I shouldn't have raised my voice.*

Kim paraphrases Simon's defense without dismissing Yvette's legitimate point:

It sounds like even though you are capable of being more thorough, you've resisted it because of your desire to spend more time with patients. What I understand from Yvette and from the doctors is that this information is critical *for making better decisions regarding patient care. What should we do to meet that need?*

Yvette acknowledges that this issue goes beyond Simon:

Well, it is not just Simon who does a mediocre job at it, I can say that for sure. Dr. Hartnett has told me that she wished everyone was as clear and precise as I am.

Kim seizes on an opportunity to include Yvette in the solution to this problem:

Would you be willing to do a staff presentation on best practices for the EMR?

Yvette demonstrates that most people want to be included and are willing to shoulder responsibility:

I would love to do it. Maybe I could talk to Dr. Hartnett about it. She knows what she needs to see.

Kim now takes the important step of making sure the agreement is carried out promptly:

Great. We will figure out a timeline once you talk to Dr. Hartnett. She usually makes her rounds first thing in the morning. Will you be here tomorrow?

Kim reinforces the importance of the idea. Then she moves to the last issue on the agenda, the one that Simon is most concerned about:

This is a high priority. It is very important that all nurses document accurately. We're making good progress. Simon, one thing that you said really captured my attention. You mentioned your frustration about focusing on charting instead of being with the patients. That is really about patient relations. *It is no secret about your reputation regarding good patient relations.*

It is Simon's turn to be the expert:

Thanks Kim. I take our mission very seriously—"quality patient care for the whole person." People are going through so much. I want to help them heal, not just physically, but emotionally too.

When Kim asks him to explain further, he continues:

Well, we are supposed to see each patient a minimum of twice during each shift. I know our vocational nurses have more patient contact, but these two times are critical. I MAKE time to talk to them about their care, I answer the questions that I can, and ask them about how they are. I spend time with them, Yvette. I don't just stare at their monitors.

Kim quickly interjects:

Thank you, Simon. This is the intention of that policy—to get the RNs on the floors to interact more with patients.

Yvette's tone is assertive but no longer as hostile:

Are you suggesting that I am not skilled in this? Well, I don't have a shrine at work honoring me so I guess I AM mediocre in that category.

Kim picks up quickly:

Our mission statement is "quality patient care for the whole person," so quality patient care means good patient relations—people skills and attentive engagement with the patient. And, utilizing that time—interacting twice per shift per patient, one at a time—Yvette, this could be an opportunity to develop better bedside nursing skills.

Then Simon chimes in:

Maybe there is a bedside nursing class in the training department, Yvette. Or maybe you can shadow me someday and see how satisfying it is when patients feel like they have your personal attention and interest. It is very gratifying.

Yvette now exhibits a different, softer side to her personality, a common change at this point simply because the conversation has been collaborative and has evolved naturally:

Well, I guess if I am telling you that you need a class, it is only fair that I'm willing to do the same, as long as it's not too touchy-feely. And I will consider the shadowing offer. I don't want patients to think of me as a cold fish.

Again, Kim seizes on a suggestion and offers a specific way it could work:

Actually, there is a new video that you can watch that discusses the key goals of our improved bedside nursing standard of care, and it gives some tips. Organizational Development did a great job with it. Yvette, would you be willing to watch it?

Now a real participant in a problem-solving conversation, Yvette responds:

Yes. I think that is a good idea, actually. It may not seem like it but I sometimes feel a bit shy in interacting with patients and their families. Perhaps I should shadow Simon; after all, he does have a shrine.

Once again, Simon speaks up in his own defense:

Excuse me, Kim, but I have to say that I resent the fact that Yvette says that I have a shrine at work. What is that supposed to mean?

Yvette is ready:

You know, the nurses' station—"Simon's Shrine."

A little embarrassed by the charge and at how others might see the situation, Simon explains:

That's supposed to be inspirational.

Yvette responds:

What is inspiring about seeing a zillion e-mails and cards about you?

Yvette is speaking for herself and the other nurses. Kim now intervenes before the conversation deteriorates. It is important that once the parties have had an opportunity to vent a little, the manager not let the conversation devolve into past blaming but move forward into the future through problem solving. To accomplish this Kim says:

It seems like Simon's intentions are to inspire good patient relations by posting patient comments but it is not having the impact that he had hoped it would, especially for you, Yvette. My concern about this is that the workstation remains clutter-free so all the nurses can work without distraction. What other options do we have to inspire nurses?

Kim is making sure that all options are considered, but also that Simon's intentions and interests in inspiring others are respected. That is an important aspect of the process—hearing and acknowledging the underlying interests behind a person's behavior and complaints. The more the manager has the ability to pick up on those needs and can acknowledge and express them as part of the problem-solving discussion, the more positive the tone of the conversation and the problem-solving discussion will be.

Now Simon asks a genuine question:

I want everyone's positive comments to get attention somehow. Could I do something to highlight that? It seems like it would encourage everyone.

As a manager, Kim has an idea and contributes to the suggestions:

What about the online newsletter? Maybe you could do a monthly column. They are always looking for good stories from the floors.

Yvette doesn't want to be left out of the problem-solving discussion, and asks:

Can't you use a bulletin board or something?

Kim reminds Simon and Yvette that she is "the boss" and that she is also supportive of the positive tone that the conversation has taken, and she adds an important comment:

You have my okay to do a bulletin board, as long as it includes cards for other nurses and you get permission from each sender to display his or her card publicly.

Kim is reminding Simon and Yvette about their responsibility to the patients as well as to their fellow nurses, who will be affected by their decision. Then once again, Kim assumes some responsibility for making sure that the workable suggestions are supported. Kim begins to suggest that they have finished the meeting, but Yvette is not quite so ready to end the discussion:

What about professional boundaries? Isn't that what we came together to talk about?

Simon acknowledges the issue:

Oh, yes, well, that is important. I think I am within the guidelines, but I don't know. I don't give patients my private address or e-mail, so all interactions are here at the hospital. But, I do get close to them.

But this issue is important to Yvette and she is not ready to let it go, though now she has a new respect for her colleague:

It is just not healthy to get so attached. It will burn you out, Simon. And you are a good nurse. I don't want you to go back to accounting.

Kim allows this interchange to occur. It demonstrates that real progress is being made. Simon responds with a slight smile:

Yvette, I never considered that might be part of your concern. Thank you. Maybe you do care about people after all . . . just kidding.

Kim again demonstrates her familiarity with available resources and her involvement in creating solutions that will benefit not only Yvette and Simon, but the whole staff:

I think we should have someone from Patient Relations talk to us about the sensitive subject of appropriate professional boundaries—balancing that with good bedside nursing care. In Geriatrics, it's an especially important issue that all nurses have to deal with. We will look at this as a possible in-service training some time. Also, HR is going to help put in place a policy that reflects an industry standard in this area; I think that will help all the nurses in this hospital. It should be published in a month or so.

Kim then begins to wind down the meeting with a question about an interest she has moving forward:

I want to remind each of you that one of the hospital's core values is teamwork. How am I going to be assured that there will be a better sense of teamwork between the two of you and that the communication between the two of you will be more professional?

Yvette's sense of humor reasserts itself, but she is sincere:

Since I am going to watch the video and shadow Simon, I am sure I will be a master at connecting . . . no, seriously, I think I have gained a better understanding of where Simon is coming from and since he is really going to make efforts to improve, I think it will just naturally get better.

Simon has a request of Yvette:

If I could ask you, Yvette, to tell me when you have a concern, that would really help me. I get very oversensitive about negative vibes; I would prefer you just come to me privately and talk nicely.

Yvette responds:

Okay, I can do that. It's a fair enough request.

Kim summarizes and then nails down important details of the agreement:

We have made tremendous progress, Yvette and Simon. You both will be learning to improve your skills in different areas. We will have two in-service trainings: one on best practices with EMR and one, at a later date, on boundaries with patients. Simon and I will talk to Lareatha [the media and public relations coordinator] *about an online column, and Yvette agrees to talk directly to Simon about any concerns she may have in the future. When will you be able to remove the cards and e-mails from the nurse's station, Simon?*

Simon responds quickly:

I can do it by tomorrow afternoon, for sure.

After working through all the details, Kim reminds them of one more joint responsibility—to their workmates:

Is there anything that we should tell the others about this meeting? Let's not forget that they have felt the tension between you lately.

Yvette is thoughtful:

The only things that I can think of are the change in cell phone policy and the fact that Simon will be making the bulletin board and starting that new column. The nurses will see that we are getting along better, I am sure of it.

Simon backs her up:

I agree. And it seems like the in-service trainings will not need to be connected to this meeting. We have those once a month or so, anyway.

Kim is now ready to end the session. Her low-key reminder about documenting the agreement is very important and will ensure that everyone is clear about what was decided together:

Okay, I think we are all in agreement. I will type up an e-mail to you both with these points specified. I will also check up with each of you in a couple of weeks to see how things have improved. Thank you for working so hard to make this successful. My expectation is that if something comes up in the future that is challenging for you two along the lines we spoke about today, you will try to work it out together and not build a wall. You are both very important to our department. Simon, before you leave, let's move to my computer to look at scheduling your IV training.

You may note that Kim deviates somewhat from her original agenda, demonstrating that the best facilitators respond to the people, not just to the plan. Having the agenda in place allows Kim to be more responsive to the flow of the conversation and the needs of the participants, so it serves as a flexible guide to the process.

PART THREE

Using The Exchange in the Workplace

CHAPTER 7

The Classic Exchange:
One Manager, Two Employees

I t had been a very hectic Monday at the clinic: appointments were running over; emergencies had taken up more time than usual and when a patient showed up over an hour late for his appointment, the front desk receptionist told him he would have to reschedule for another day. When John Chu, the physician's assistant (PA) who had been scheduled to meet with the patient, heard that the appointment had been canceled, he erupted in anger in front of a waiting room full of patients. The receptionist, Lilly Brown, had burst into tears and called Drew Thompson, head of Employee Relations, about filing a grievance.

Recognizing that there was more to know about the situation, and aware that both employees were generally good workers, Drew suggested to Lilly that a first step in the hospital's policy was an opportunity to take part in an Exchange session. He arranged to meet with Lilly later that afternoon. (He also agreed to make arrangements with her supervisor to cover her workstation during that time.) And he stopped by the PA's office to schedule a private meeting with John before he went off duty.

In the previous part of the book, we examined each stage of The Exchange in detail, with an extended example. This chapter looks at a second example of the classic Exchange, in which the manager meets with two employees to resolve issues around their working relationship. Information is presented in a comprehensive way and summarizes the important aspects of the process, its stages, and some useful techniques. In later chapters, we will explore variations and adaptations of The Exchange that managers have found to be helpful.

The Exchange is a key early option for managers facing a conflict under their watch. It can be initiated by:

▸ The manager who becomes aware of the problem.

▸ One of the involved parties who asks for it.

▸ A person in authority who asks a manager to conduct the process.

CONVENING THE EXCHANGE

The convener of The Exchange needs to be someone who is respected by both parties. It should also be someone who has ties to those involved and is a normal part of the chain of command. If the power distance between the parties and the convener is too great—if, for example, Radha Samson herself or even Drew Thompson had conducted the earlier process—the process would likely have taken on the aura of being a disciplinary session, regardless of what had been said to deny it. In such a situation the parties are often "infantilized" and simply wait for the "boss" to tell them what to do rather than take responsibility themselves. They lose a little face by having someone much further up in the hierarchy call attention to the incident by getting directly involved.

Instead, the convener should be someone who holds at least a slightly higher position than the parties to the dispute but ideally someone who works within the department or area and is familiar with both employees. This gives legitimacy to the process and invests the facilitator with important procedural authority. The convener in a classic Exchange has a personal stake in the outcome of the process; its success reflects on the department and on the manager, who has the chance to enhance a reputation for fairness and quick action.

How quick? Not every dispute or disagreement in a hospital needs The Exchange. Competent individuals can and do disagree and experience personality clashes that they can deal with and move on with their responsibilities. It's when a situation doesn't blow over and begins to affect collaborative work or department morale that it is important to address it through The Exchange.

In any workplace, particular individuals often function as de facto conciliators and every manager benefits from such people. But when a problem between employees affects or threatens to affect the whole department, it needs to be addressed by someone with organizational and personal authority. Here are some examples:

▶ A physician lead or the Chief Medical Officer of a hospital would probably be the person to convene a case of a personality clash between a cardiologist and a hospitalist.

▶ The director of Food Services would be the appropriate person to initiate The Exchange between two cafeteria workers.

▶ Kim Brown, a head nurse in an important wing of the hospital, was the perfect person to convene the dispute between her two nurses, Yvette and Simon, detailed in the preceding chapters.

In the scheduling situation at the beginning of this chapter, Drew Thompson as head of Employee Relations was the appropriate person; both involved hospital personnel who worked in the same clinic yet the clinic director had not yet learned The Exchange process. Sometimes staff members of Employee Relations conduct The Exchange when the manager isn't able or capable of doing so. They also manage conflict in departments when the manager is part of the problem.

PREPARING TO CONDUCT THE EXCHANGE

Once the convener is on board, he or she will want to do a little preparation before beginning The Exchange process. The convener should be someone familiar enough with the work schedules of the parties to be able to schedule Stage One (the private meetings) at times when the employees will normally be available and then to schedule Stage Three (the joint meeting) when both have openings in their schedules. In the healthcare setting, it is not unusual because of varying shifts for the two individuals to not be scheduled together again for some time. That is why, for example, Kim Brown chose to do the whole process in one day, at the beginning and end of the shift. In this way, the conflict wasn't left suspended for a week. In office settings with more routine work schedules, managers often hold Stage One on one day (then developing Stage Two, their agenda, on their own later that same day) and Stages Three and Four the next day so the participants have time to reflect on the initial conversation and prepare themselves mentally for the joint meeting. It's a good idea to make the first contact as informal as possible: in person or by phone. E-mail is dangerous because one can't control who might see it. While transparency is important, the invitation should not sound like discipline is entailed. Say something like:

> *We need to talk about the incident at the clinic yesterday. Are you available at 2:00 this afternoon, just before you leave for the day? I'd like to hear how you view the situation. I'll check with your supervisor and make sure you can get off early.*

Or:

> *Before it gets any more complicated, I'd like to convene an Exchange process with you and Lilly about yesterday's incident at the clinic. I'd like to talk with you about your perspective. I know you get off at 2:30. I'll check with your supervisor and make sure you can get off around 2:00.*

CHOOSING WHO TO MEET WITH FIRST

Since the separate meetings are designed to gather information for the joint session, it really doesn't matter who you meet with first. Some managers prefer to meet with the person who seems to have the most investment in the complaint. In the example at the clinic that would probably be the front-desk receptionist, Lilly. It also makes sense to begin with her since she was the one who had contacted the Employee Relations Department. The most important thing for the convener is not to buy into either presentation but to describe these preliminary meetings as opportunities to find out more about the parties and the problem.

STAGE ONE: DISCOVERING THEIR INTERESTS AND BUILDING TRUST

One of the benefits of Stage One, when you meet privately with each employee, is that the convener has a chance to build some trust with each party; this will help the joint session be productive. Trust can't be demanded; it comes from experience with another person over time and it is most likely to grow if someone believes that he or she is being dealt with fairly and honestly by another who genuinely wishes to help with a difficult situation. The one-on-one dynamic of the private meeting is conducive to creating a climate of trust. Part of the trust building lies in the convener discovering two key things:

▶ How the individual is being affected by the conflict.

▶ What that person really needs or wants from the other for there to be a resolution; this is the individual's *real interest*.

The individual's real interest may be as simple as respect from the other person or as complicated as a fair division of labor for the whole department. It is almost always couched in a complaint:

I wasn't treated the way I should have been by the other person, who should have known better.

The facilitator's job is to reframe the negative complaint into a more neutral statement of what is wanted. Being able to determine and articulate what each person wants or needs rather than what they *didn't get* is an important skill.

During his meeting with Lilly, Drew learned that she had felt humiliated by the reaction of the Physician's Assistant, who had not asked the receptionist what had happened before lecturing her in a very loud voice in front of a waiting room full of patients. He had accused her of arbitrarily undermining the doctor-patient relationship and of not doing her job. Lilly's interest, what she wanted, was to be treated respectfully.

What John, the PA, didn't know was that Lilly, the receptionist, had been working two shifts because another receptionist had called in sick at the last moment. He also seemed unaware of all the patients who were on time and waiting for their appointments; everyone had been waiting for at least a half hour. What he also didn't know was that his patient had broken in to the front of the waiting line and demanded an appointment immediately.

Drew also learned some important pieces of information from the John, the PA. He discovered that John had a long-term relationship with this particular patient and understood that the man had great difficulty getting anywhere—he had no car or money for a taxi and was dependent on public transportation. On that day his bus had broken down and made all the passengers late. At that day's appointment the PA had hoped to give his patient some simple tests and exercises to alleviate his chronic condition and realized that now the man would need to go through the whole transportation rigmarole again. He was very committed to his patients and hoped some day to become a hospitalist. *John Chu's interest was to provide the quality care he knew the patient needed without interference from the scheduler.* John also had had a frustrating day of what seemed like bureaucratic snags and incompetence and he had snapped when the event occurred. He was embarrassed to have lost his temper but defensive about why he had.

STAGE TWO: PLANNING AN AGENDA

After talking to each party, the facilitator constructs an agenda for Stage Two, the joint meeting. As described earlier in the book, the agenda should include an *icebreaker*, a discussion of the *impact*, and a list of *issues* that need to be addressed in the session.

While thinking and planning alone in Stage Two, think about the personalities of the participants and what kind of questions about impact might work for them. One women's healthcare clinic manager said:

I am just going to ask them how they feel about what happened. We talk about feelings all the time in our clinic.

This made the manager of the hospital fleet laugh and remark:

Not in my department, I think that they would look at me like I was from another planet. "How has it been working together?" definitely would work better with my department.

You know your employees. Consider them as you form your *impact* question.

After he had talked with both employees, Drew took a few minutes to review what he had heard and developed an agenda for the joint meeting, which was scheduled for the next morning. He realized that both the PA and the receptionist had been under unusual stress imposed by conditions outside their control and that both had demonstrated commitment to their jobs throughout the incident:

▶ Lilly had stepped in for a colleague and thought she was making things easier on the doctors, nurses, and physician assistants, who were already overbooked with patients.

▶ John had gone out of his way to have the latest studies available for his patient and had looked forward to making life easier for him.

What was missing, Drew thought, was a clinic-wide protocol for dealing with latecomers. This was something he could help with when they met. He also realized that both employees needed to hear how the other had experienced the incident before any solution could be found. His agenda of topics for the joint meeting includes:

▶ How to deal with unexpected situations at the front desk (*issue*)

▶ Protocols to follow when there is a problem (*issue*)

▶ The effect of this situation on both parties and the clinic staff (*impact*)

▶ How each saw his/her role in relation to the hospital's mission (*icebreaker*)

Notice that Drew first planned the two issues. Then he thought about the way he would ask about the impact of the situation. Finally, he thought about an icebreaker. Most managers find that thinking about topics in that order works the best in the Stage Two planning phase. It is natural to figure out what needs to be fixed first (*issues*) and then do the planning for the other two topics after that.

But in the actual Stage Three discussion, the rollout will be in reverse:

- ▶ First, discuss the *icebreaker* (after the manager makes introductory comments about the process).

- ▶ Second, discuss the *impact*.

- ▶ Third, move to the *issues*, one at a time.

Throughout the joint discussion, Drew listened carefully for the underlying interests of Lilly and John, which are often unspoken. Facilitators of the process become adept at listening on several levels: for the facts, the impact, and the interests. A skilled facilitator often uncovers those underlying interests and reinforces them in a variety of ways. In this situation, after Drew heard Lilly complain about "how rude John was," he commented that "it sounds like it is important to you that you are treated respectfully." Later, when John complained that "Lilly just made up her own mind about when someone was too late," Drew asked, "Am I correct that both of you are hoping for more clear expectations about what to do in these situations?" Drew was also clear about the clinic's interests, stating those as needed. The power of this way of speaking helps the participants view each other, the situation, and the possible solutions in a far different light.

STAGES THREE AND FOUR: ANALYZING THE ISSUES AND BUILDING AN AGREEMENT

In the best of circumstances, Stages Three and Four feel like a three-way conversation with everyone participating and working together to problem solve. Most often, the manager needs to take a strong leadership role, ensuring that people are treated respectfully and monitoring the exchange of information so that each party really understands the message sent by the other. Where there is most likely to be a barrier in communicating is when the parties talk to each other about how they were affected by the situation. This impact that each is feeling is often what has blocked any progress before the conflict ensued and will continue to create problems unless it can be put on the table. An impact cannot be "fixed." But it *can* be talked about, carefully.

Exchanging information about feelings or emotions may make people feel vulnerable, so they are often reluctant to do so. One of the manager's jobs is to help the parties frame this important information in terms that preserve each party's dignity and demonstrate that each has been affected. We have found that finding words other than "feelings" or "emotions" is helpful. Try:

Obviously, that situation has taken its toll on both of you. Could you talk about that a little?

Or:

So how has this situation affected your work life?

Or:

I can sense from talking to each of you that this situation has had a big effect on all of us. It would be helpful to hear briefly how you have been affected.

Then, after each of them has spoken, say:

For my part, I have noticed that some other staff members have not been able to focus on their jobs as much as they normally do because this situation is affecting the whole clinic staff. I am concerned that it not spill over and affect the way our patients view us.

Once the impact of the dispute has been exchanged between the parties, the facilitator begins the discussion about the issues, which leads naturally into Stage Four. As described in the previous part of the book the manager:

- ▶ Raises an issue.

- ▶ Allows each employee to state his or her perspective on the topic.

- ▶ Acknowledges those perspectives.

- ▶ Sets forth his or her own expectations (if any).

Then they all work together on possible solutions in Stage Four.

When you conduct an Exchange, you will notice at this point that there is a new atmosphere in the room. The hard things have been spoken of and there is relief at beginning to think about solutions. One at a time, the parties talk about each issue and then decide together what to do about each one. A convenient guide is:

- ▶ **Define.** It should be clear what is meant by each issue. For example, what "late for an appointment" means probably needs to be spelled out. Is late 15 minutes or 5 minutes? What are acceptable exceptions?

- ▶ **Discuss.** Using the waiting room incident as a concrete example, the PA and the receptionist each get an opportunity to talk about what they expected of the other when the patient was late.

- ▶ **Determine interests.** After acknowledging the employee perspectives and interests, the manager addresses any workplace expectations around the topic.

- ▶ **Decide.** Examine the possible solutions to remedy the situation. Was this a one-time incident or something that happens often? Is there a hard-and-fast rule or some flexibility? How would each party want to handle the situation should it occur again? How will other staffers react to this decision? How will they know about it?

- ▶ **Document.** Writing down decisions, either as memoranda or as an agreement, will avoid misunderstandings later. Many managers find writing an e-mail after the session is the best way to document the session. It clarifies what was decided, yet still has the tone of informality. It will also be a useful tool for the manager to use to measure future improvement. Whatever the format, the document is written with participation from everyone. Everyone should be clear about the documentation and know where it will be kept and who will have access to it.

Then the session is over! We recommend a formal ending that includes kudos for the work accomplished and encouragement to uphold commitments.

Not all conflicts are so neat. Often conflicts involve three or many more people. Some conflicts involve only one person. We will address this last situation first. But we hope it will be clear that the basic structure for dealing with the conflict remains the same and that the techniques used are effective ones.

8

Adapting The Exchange to Manage a Disruptive Employee

It can happen in any workplace. Sometimes one person seems to be at the center of, or a participant in, every conflict. These individuals often wield more power than their position warrants; other employees tend to avoid them or give in to what they demand in order to avoid an argument. Occasionally a disruptive employee is even unaware of what is happening.

A surgeon at St. Sonia's Hospital noticed that while hospital policy encouraged teams to work as a unit and thereby build trust and rapport, his team was constantly changing except for the scrub nurse, a tall, tough former medic. The surgeon was frustrated about having to "teach" a new group every time he was scheduled for surgery and finally, after an operation, he asked the nurse what was going on. The nurse stepped back, put his hands on his hips, and said, "I'm the only one who can stand working with you." The surgeon was shocked and asked for more information. He eventually acknowledged that his abrupt style could be seen as demeaning and also that what he really wanted was to develop a strong team with the best reputation possible but that his style had prevented it. It took some work, and more "coaching" from the scrub nurse, but eventually the surgeon met his own interest of having a team that worked well together and even liked each other!

Most of the time there is not an ex-Marine to stand up to the disruptive individual who causes misery for everyone in the department. Then it becomes the responsibility of an administrator, a department head, or the Employee Assistance Program to do something about the situation.

But bad behavior often goes unaddressed and the excuse will be made, "Everyone is entitled to a bad day." This may be true. But when the bad day turns into a pattern of disruptive behavior or ongoing disrespect to coworkers, then a different approach is needed. Managers often move from avoiding the situation to attacking through discipline procedures, often wanting to fire the person immediately without following the progressive intermediate steps required. The reason for this is simple: these meetings are challenging.

REASONS FOR USING THE EXCHANGE WITH A DISRUPTIVE EMPLOYEE

Since replacing a talented employee is not easy or without significant financial cost, it is often worth the time and effort to address the issue head-on. While not a classic example of a case for The Exchange, the structure and the techniques of the process are still applicable, with a few tweaks. The Exchange methodology gives managers the opportunity to deal with such situations successfully.

Using The Exchange conveys the unspoken message to the entire staff that the administration cares about the atmosphere of the workplace and will work with individuals who do not follow basic rules of civil behavior toward their colleagues. The Exchange is a nonthreatening way to examine a difficult situation and explore options that will be satisfactory to everyone.

Disruptive employees have often had many unpleasant encounters with others and are used to being treated as pariahs. In The Exchange they have the chance to talk and explain how they see the situation, not just respond to charges or complaints.

Using The Exchange with a disruptive employee can give the manager clear guidelines for the discussion points and some techniques that work well in other conflict situations. The task is to have a productive encounter that results in bettering a difficult situation. This will take planning, self-discipline, and strategy. Knowledge of the stages of The Exchange will be a great help.

A typical case was the one that Radha Samson planned to deal with as her last appointment of the day, a situation with the information technology (IT) technician, Brian Jones, referred to privately as "The Wiz." Radha had received numerous complaints about Brian. Basically, his job was that of a computer troubleshooter. He was in charge of updating computers throughout the hospital. There seemed to be no glitches he couldn't fix, no program he wasn't familiar with, and no job too simple or too complex. Unfortunately, his social skills did not match his technical skills. A few examples:

▶ Last week, in front of other employees, Brian had informed a program manager in Aging Services who was struggling with a new computer that *any idiot should be able to figure out this program.* The program manager had been so upset with Brian's behavior and the way his boss had ignored her concerns that she cried during her phone call to Radha to complain about the incident. Upon inquiring of various staff, Radha learned that several of them avoided contacting Brian because they didn't like being "yelled at."

▶ Two weeks ago, an undergraduate intern had changed a password on a computer in Admin without informing IT and when Brian came to fix it, he announced in a loud voice, *"All such students are just a waste of time and probably shouldn't even have access to computers."* Other staffers were shocked but reluctant to confront Brian. Radha heard about the incident during a regular check-in with the department.

▶ Most recently, a physician who the hospital hoped to hire was touring the facility and visited IT. He noted that the department seemed to be quite sophisticated. At that point Brian jumped into the conversation, uninvited. He pointed out that the newest models could do a lot more, and then said with a grin, *"You have a lot of money; why don't you buy us all new computers?"* When the embarrassed physician demurred, Brian muttered in a barely audible tone, *"Rich people—you're all alike."* Later in the day the physician turned down Radha's offer of a position at the hospital and during the course of their conversation mentioned the incident.

Radha called Brian's supervisor, Francisco, who said he would rather focus on Brian's technical skills than his social skills. The supervisor admitted to having received complaints from other departments and knew that most of his colleagues were leery of speaking up to Brian because they didn't want to deal with his biting sarcasm. Everyone was aware that a year ago Brian had saved the hospital's computer system from a potentially deadly virus that would have disrupted a key record-keeping system. Brian had quickly researched the virus and was able to install a protective system, one he now would need to train all employees to use. He was an important asset—and he was impossible to work with. Radha decided that Brian's role was important enough to warrant her intervention and decided to use The Exchange as a vehicle. Her other option was a disciplinary session, which she knew would likely end in an escalation of the tension surrounding Brian and possibly in his firing (in which case she would need to work with the Employee Association). Or he might just quit and St. Sonia's Hospital would lose his unique skills. She invited Brian's supervisor to participate in the session so that he could learn about The Exchange techniques while he took part in the discussion.

ADJUSTING THE EXCHANGE PROCESS FOR DEALING WITH ONE EMPLOYEE

While key elements of The Exchange structure remain the same, there are differences in using the process to manage one person compared to dealing with a classic two-party conflict. The obvious major change is that the facilitator, or Radha, in this case, begins with Stage Two, the agenda-planning phase. In this instance, Radha knew enough detail about specific incidents through complaints from several sources that she was able to strategize a plan to deal with Brian in one session through a meld of Stages One, Three, and Four. This one-session approach is typical in many of these situations.

RADHA SAMSON USING THE EXCHANGE WITH IT TECHNICIAN BRIAN JONES

Here is how Radha conducted The Exchange with Brian. Radha began with a clear description of the purpose of the meeting, her interest in working through the issues, and the goal of developing a plan with Brian to improve the situation. She stressed that this was not a disciplinary session; her hope was to manage the situation so that discipline would not be necessary.

This tone setting and clarifying of the discussion parameters at the beginning of the meeting help the facilitator achieve the needed results. Managers tell us that planning their agenda ahead of time and having a checklist of topics to cover really helps them begin the meeting with more confidence.

In her *opening statement*, Radha told Brian that they would really need to talk about how he worked with others in the hospital and how he communicated with the staff. Before she began talking about the *issues* with Brian, she complimented him on his technology skills and asked him how he got into his specialization (the *icebreaker*). Although Brian had the reputation of being a very difficult person, he obviously enjoyed having the opportunity to talk about himself. Radha followed up by asking what his thoughts were when she approached him about his dealings with colleagues (the *impact* on him) and she got an earful. She did everything she could to *acknowledge* him and to make sure he knew she wanted to understand his perspective. Before talking about her point of view, she used appropriate body language to show that she was paying attention as Brian stated his perspective. When he was finished, she *summarized* his key points until he was satisfied that he had been heard. Employees like Brian are often individuals who are not used to being listened to; other people don't like them and avoid engaging in any conversation at all, let alone a conversation about touchy issues. To have someone, especially someone higher up in the organization, actually encourage him or her to talk and then demonstrate that she was listening is unbalancing to his or her natural defensiveness.

After that, she spoke about the effects of his behavior on his coworkers. She was careful to frame the description factually and not seem to attack him. In this way, she was describing the impact from the perspective of others. In the discussion of the *issues,* Brian participated by offering what information Radha had, and together they decided what to do next.

It wasn't an easy conversation; Radha was challenged several times. She got sidetracked for a while because Brian blamed everyone else for his behavior and she found herself getting diverted and seeming to agree about *how oversensitive everyone* was. It is one thing to take into consideration the other person's perspective. It is quite another to be derailed into agreeing with it or trying to fix everyone and everything else. Once she realized what was happening she said:

> *Perhaps these things wouldn't upset you, but I am telling you that this is a pattern of behavior with a wide range of people, not just one. And, whether you think they are being oversensitive or not, we need to find some alternative ways for you to demonstrate a modicum of respect for colleagues who need your technical assistance. You have a lot to offer them; there is no doubt about it. We just need to find ways that the other part doesn't get in the way of their learning.*

At one point during the conversation Radha realized that she was being overcontrolling as she tried to maintain the boundaries of the conversation. Brian began to be agitated, so she paused for a moment and acknowledged how challenging it was, how frustrated he was, and that he truly did have a lot to offer the hospital. She saw an immediate shift in his demeanor as he became calmer and more cooperative.

Radha and Brian worked to resolve the issues around his tone with other employees. She also took into consideration Brian's complaint that he had shown the employee in Aging Services how to operate the same system many times. She would call the IT department insisting there was something wrong with her computer or the particular program, but the problem was always user error. Radha reminded him that his calling the woman an "idiot" was obviously uncalled for and clearly unprofessional, but she was also ready to look at his point of view and consider it when they got to Stage Four, Problem Solving. Radha's willingness to do this made all the difference to Brian.

Along with Brian's supervisor, Francisco, they planned that when Brian was called to fix something that wasn't broken, but stemmed from a lack of understanding on the part of the user, he would simply acknowledge to the coworker that it was a challenging program (even if he didn't think it was!). Brian would explain that although he understood the program, he found it difficult to make its proper use clear to others. So they developed a video in the Training Department for Brian to review. Providing Brian with some ready-made phrases gave him tools to help control his knee-jerk negative reactions. Brian's supervisor was a key part of the conversation. He agreed to check in with Brian more often to make sure things were on track.

After Brian left, his supervisor shared that watching Radha handle The Exchange session so professionally made it seem much more manageable. He had been afraid to address these issues with Brian, but the strategy and techniques he learned now gave him more confidence.

At times, however, an employee like Brian is not prepared to move from Stage Three to Stage Four and talk about solutions. A disruptive employee may have a personality that prevents him or her from engaging in much self-reflection. Such individuals do not respond to blame or accusations and they may have a heightened sense of being victims or of being judged unfairly. But they will often respond to boundaries that are larger than the two people in the room, such as hospital policies or disciplinary structures over which neither of them has control. Part of Radha's or the facilitator's job is to make sure that the individual understands the likely result of violating such hospital policies or standards.

Other times, an employee just needs time to reflect on what he or she has heard. In such a situation a manager will find it helpful to give the employee time, tell him or her that they both will benefit from a day or so to think about the conversation that has transpired, and that each should come back at a later date prepared to discuss specific options. It goes without saying that this will be done without attacking, blaming, or threatening the employee. If a second session is warranted, it should be scheduled as soon as possible so that the momentum of the first session is not lost.

The employee and the facilitator look together at the solutions available to resolve the situation. It is critical that the disruptive employee make commitments about what he or she is willing to do to improve. And it is important that these commitments be written down and the document signed by both parties. No threats are made in the course of this problem solving session but the consequences attached to future negative behaviors should be clearly spelled out and these should be seen as incentives for the employee to live up to their joint agreement.

In the most difficult situation where the disruptive individual seems unable to agree to adjust his or her behavior, the conversation may conclude with a discussion of the steps the manager plans to take to provide a remedy. The manager can state that he or she believes the employee has the ability to be part of the problem-solving process but if the employee chooses not to be, the manager has the responsibility, for the well-being of the department, to make sure the issue is addressed. It is only after this conversation that a disciplinary approach might be necessary.

Using The Exchange with a disruptive employee helps the facilitator challenge the individual's habitual pattern. The facilitator's active listening to, and acknowledgment of, the employee encourages the employee to lower his or her defenses. The facilitator offers the employee the chance to try a more productive way of interacting and to choose a new path, rather than being stifled by an old, unproductive one.

CHAPTER 9

The Exchange Aikidoist: How to Use the Techniques When You Are Attacked

In this chapter, we will focus more on The Exchange *techniques* than on the formal process. How can we use the techniques central to The Exchange in everyday encounters, for instance, when one of our colleagues attacks us? If the person is our subordinate, perhaps we can use the hierarchical relationship or discipline to manage the situation. But what if that person is our peer or above us in the organization?

Early in his career in Employee Relations (before he became the director) Drew Thompson was surprised one day when his coworker, Sylvia, came into his office yelling:

How dare you e-mail me about the event last night and copy our boss! You have no right to make me look bad like that!

She was known to have a temper. Drew was surprised that someone who was such an expert at helping other employees could be so difficult to work with on a daily basis. The coworker seemed to have no problem in assessing other people's situations and dispensing advice, but she often reacted emotionally when it was her own issues. Clearly he had done something wrong in her book, so he focused on trying to understand what her concerns were. He recognized that it was not about him, per se; it was more about him violating an important need that she had. Drew took a deep breath and remembered to take an Aikido approach.

In the world of marital arts, Aikido is the one most metaphorically applicable to general conflict resolution and specifically to working with high-conflict individuals. We begin here with the Aikido philosophy to plan our response. A manager will find the mind-set of an Aikidoist to be very helpful.

AIKIDO AND THE EXCHANGE

First, here are some comments about Aikido. It is a defensive art. The Aikidoist does not seek conflict, but also does not fear it or run from it. Rather he or she prepares for it in a careful, disciplined way. It is an art that requires the practitioner to be centered and calm. In other words, the practitioner is taught to be able to *respond* and not to *react*. *Reacting* is an instinctive action that all too often gives control to the attacker. *Responding* is a thoughtful action *chosen* by the Aikidoist. Responding is done in a measured, careful way: the situation does not escalate and no one is harmed. To accomplish this, an Aikidoist throws his or her opposite off balance—without hurting the person—to give the person a different view of the situation. This is exactly what needs to happen when you are on the receiving end of a verbal attack.

Why should you take an Aikido approach when you feel attacked? Consider your *other* options. You can:

▶ *Avoid the person or give in.* The problem with this approach is that the other person learns that confrontation with you works well, and you also will not get your own needs met.

▶ *Counterattack to raise the ante of who has more power, formal or informal.* Counterattacking may be even more risky because the high-conflict person has practice in his or her approach; it has worked for him or her in the past. By reacting, you have, in a sense, given the high-conflict person the power to control you. This is tricky business.

The Aikido philosophy doesn't accept either of these two extremes. It means not having to win or show your power in that moment. It means putting a *pause* between action and response. It is probably one of the hardest things a quick-thinking person needs to learn, yet, we would contend, it is very much worth the challenge. The potential gain is worth the effort. As William Ury wrote in his book *Getting Past No: Negotiating from Confrontation to Cooperation* (New York: Bantam, 1993), "Don't get mad, don't get even, get what you want." That is exactly what the Aikido approach does for you; it helps you stay rooted in your real interests instead of being diverted into petty fighting. Once you have found the pause button within yourself and have learned not to say the first thing that comes to mind, you may wonder: What should I do next?

This is where The Exchange techniques can really work for you. Much of this book has been dedicated to the techniques of *effectively listening, responding respectfully,* and *asking questions* (see especially Appendix A for complete descriptions). These are the perfect responses to an attack. By doing these techniques you demonstrate that you really want to understand the other person's perspective.

The reality is that you may not like the other person, the way he or she approaches you, or his or her style of communicating, but the other person is trying to get across to you something about which he or she feels strongly. If you can remain curious about the *content*, not be thrown by the other person's *delivery* (by making use of the Aikido stance!), wonder what is going on for the other person, and be open to his or her perspective, it will help you utilize The Exchange skills.

The ability to depersonalize the attack helps. Many times it has more to do with the attacker's needs than a shortcoming in you. Relaxed open body language and a willingness to listen convey the seriousness with which you take the other person's concerns. If you react in your body and you appear defensive or hostile, it will only escalate emotions.

Even if you think you are in the right in the situation, take the time to appreciate the other person's perspective and let him or her know what you understand. Acknowledge the other person's feelings in a way that is not patronizing.

DREW THOMPSON USING THE AIKIDO APPROACH

As mentioned earlier, Drew once made a mistake with a coworker, Sylvia. He sent her an e-mail and copied their boss. Sylvia went on a bit of a rant and became quite agitated. Drew's pause button was functioning well for him and he tried to display an open stance with her. It all seemed to be working well until he acknowledged the coworker in a calm voice. The coworker yelled:

Don't you patronize me. This is a serious issue!

Drew was baffled at what had gone wrong. He was able to work through it but reflecting on it later he realized his mistake. His calm, quiet voice had been too much of a contrast to the coworker's angry loud one. It was still Drew's goal to have a calmer discussion of the concerns but this time he started her *acknowledgment* loudly, slowly lowering the energy and the decibel level of his voice:

I CAN SEE THIS IS VERY IMPORTANT TO YOU! You were really upset with me about sending that e-mail to you. . . .

Her response this time was to actually calm down a bit and assert, "*Exactly!*" Inwardly relieved, Drew still didn't tell his perspective; he followed that up with an open-ended question:

Tell me more about what my doing that *meant for you.*

It is probably most important to hear not just the complaints but also the interests and workplace needs of the other person. The more you respond to the person's needs and interests, instead of reacting to the attack, the better able you are to transform the conversation.

What doesn't work is to tell the person that he or she is too angry and not being reasonable, because this is really a veiled attack which escalates the situation, or to give an excuse or blame the other person. In other words, you shouldn't say, "*If this has happened before, you should have told me this sooner instead of letting it build up.*"

Drew really attempted to listen beyond the words she was saying to her underlying *interests.* After listening further, he reflected back:

You would have wanted me to talk to you personally and directly about the situation. Your reputation with our boss is important to you.

The tone of the conversation should be a bit calmer now after a few minutes of focused listening and responding respectfully. If you truly are listening and responding respectfully—demonstrating understanding, acknowledging feelings, and identifying the person's interests—yet nothing helps, maybe it is time to take a break. You should acknowledge that this is a lot of information for you and you want some time to think about it, or to say that both of you are pretty upset.

Assuming that the techniques work, as they usually do, what happens next? Drew insists that he never calls them *techniques*; he says they help him *listen* better, not manipulate the other person for his own purposes. Does that mean you're done? The other person feels better and you truly understand his or her concerns. As you probably guessed, there is more to it.

What about *your* perspective? After hearing your coworker's perspective and calming down the situation, it is time to voice your perspective in a nonconfrontational way. Learning to do this by stating your *needs* can be a powerful tool. Drew tried to utilize this language on an ongoing basis, which is why he has such a good reputation in the workplace.

One thing that is important for me is that we have good teamwork in the department, so my reason for sending you the e-mail was to quickly let you know something about what happened on Thursday evening. I see now it wasn't the best approach, but my intentions were. . . .

Taking responsibility for your errors, and clearly stating your needs and interests in the situation, is an important part of the discussion. It's not all about the other person!

After you have clarified your perspective in a nonconfrontational way, work with the other person in Stage Four, the problem-solving part of the strategy. If you have ever been called stubborn, let that work for you here. Persevere in your attempts to work through the issue, being willing to say:

How do you want me to communicate my concerns to you in the future? I can see the e-mail didn't work, so let's figure this out.

The ART (*A*ikido in Action, *R*espond Respectfully, and *T*roubleshoot Together) of communication helps The Exchange and its adaptations work well. Whenever you have the need to approach someone else with a concern, using an ARTful approach will help you work through the issues and strengthen your relationship.

10

Using The Exchange to Coach an Employee When Bosses Are Bullies

Bosses who are bullies or tyrants may be liabilities to the institutions for which they work. Complaints occasionally escalate into lawsuits about unfair labor practices; charges are made of discrimination, wrongful termination, or unlawful discharge. But in too many workplaces, bully bosses are too powerful or too essential to the institution to be challenged. As a result they continue, sometimes for years, to make life miserable for those who work under them. For employees, these bosses are disastrous to morale and productivity. No one doubts that it is hard for people to work at their best when they feel unvalued and are treated disrespectfully, but it is not always clear what to do.

THE ADVANTAGES OF USING THE EXCHANGE
WITH VICTIMS OF BULLY BOSSES

While the classic Exchange process itself may not be the vehicle for working with victims of bully bosses, techniques from The Exchange can be helpful. The focused attention of a private meeting, the demonstrated understanding of a non-judgmental paraphrase, and the power of a sincere acknowledgment are all helpful in de-escalating the high emotions that these employees are living with.

Being helped to realistically examine their options enables employees who are victims of bully bosses to make choices that support their interests and that promise relief from the ongoing stress of the status quo. Often the sense of there being no choices and of being powerless is what has paralyzed the employee. Plans for the future or new projects have been put on hold and an accompanying sense of the futility of doing anything can mire one into depression. Having a reasoned discussion with a trained Exchange facilitator may go a long way to restoring the employee's sense of competence. Making a decision allows the employee to begin the rest of his or her life.

CONSIDERATIONS FOR USING THE EXCHANGE WITH AN EMPLOYEE AND A BULLY BOSS

How can The Exchange be used to deal with the huge power imbalance between a bully boss and an employee? It depends on a number of circumstances, including:

▸ Who wants the process—the boss or the employee?

▸ What is the realistic prognosis that the boss will be open to change?

▸ What will happen to the employee if there is no change in the status quo?

▸ How much power does the boss have?

▸ Can the boss fire the employee?

▸ Who is the boss's boss?

Esther Cabrera, an employee in the Food Services Department at St. Sonia's Hospital, was facing a dilemma in regard to her "bully boss," Emily Smith. At the suggestion of a coworker after a recent incident, she called Drew Johnson, her voice shaking with the stress she was under. His reputation for fairness as director of Employee Relations gave Esther some faint hope that the situation could be improved. Her hope was that Mr. Johnson would hear her out, realize how bad the situation was, and tell her boss to change.

Esther has worked for the Food Services Department for six years. Her boss, Emily Smith, had at one time been a colleague and a friend.

They lived in neighboring areas and often carpooled to work and to soccer games since their daughters played on the same team.

But when Emily was promoted to head of the Food Services Department, she seemed to undergo a personality change. She was no longer the accessible, friendly coworker but a micromanager who allowed for no discussion. It was always her way or no way. The 25 employees in the department (cooks, servers, preparers) lived in fear of being shouted at or required to perform duties outside their job description, including taking on assignments that seemed unnecessary or demeaning. Emily's reputation was that of a rule-bound director who never complimented anyone and saw only problems, which she pointed out loudly and critically for all around to hear.

Esther, who was in charge of salads and desserts, thought she might be developing an ulcer because of the stress; her stomach sometimes hurt so much that she called in sick. Lately it seemed that Emily was increasingly to pick on her. In the latest incident, she had made Esther pick out all the radicchio from the evening's salad buffet because she thought it was "too bitter" to be served with butter lettuce.

According to Esther, she had added the radicchio in order to give color and texture to a rather bland combination of more traditional greens. She had thought she was doing something helpful and felt battered when Emily yelled at her, insinuating that Esther was purposely serving something "inedible" and not in the regular recipe for the evening salad.

Situations such as this one present a dilemma for a convener of The Exchange. While there is clearly a conflict in which someone feels disrespected, there is a strong possibility that a meeting at which the two parties talk might actually *increase* the tension between them. The boss would view the employee as a tattletale who got her in trouble and therefore even more deserving of constant supervision and criticism. It is a loss of face for a boss to be contacted by an administrator because of an employee's complaint. Often, the complaints involve situations that are technically within the purview of the boss rather than being violations of actual policy.

So what does the administrator do? The administrator starts with Stage One, a one-on-one Exchange meeting, to listen to the employee's point of view. It should be noted that this is different from when the manager already has a series of issues as described previously. In that case the manager begins in Stage 2 to develop the agenda because the manager is initiating the meeting with the disruptive employee. In this case, when an employee has approached the administrator, the first task for the administrator is to learn what the issues are that are of concern to the employee. The structure of Stage 1 establishes the meeting professionally (rather than a gossip session.)

STAGE ONE BETWEEN DREW THOMPSON AND FOOD SERVICES EMPLOYEE ESTHER CABRERA

When Esther entered Drew's office, she walked in hesitantly and made only sporadic eye contact. It was apparent that she was uncomfortable and fearful of being overheard. Drew made a point of standing up and offering her a cup of coffee as a way of saying, *"Relax. It's safe here."* He quickly assured her that he would not repeat anything she said unless he had her permission. Then he asked her to tell him about the situation.

After listening, Drew made sure that he understood the employee's concerns. Drew asked Esther some questions.

DREW: *Do you want to stay in your job?*

ESTHER: *Not if Emily doesn't change.*

DREW: *Is it likely that Emily will change?*

ESTHER: *No.*

DREW: *What did you already try to do to remedy the situation?*

ESTHER: *I tried to talk to Emily, who refused to talk. I talked to other coworkers, but they felt too intimidated to speak up.*

DREW: *What is the effect of the situation on you?*

ESTHER: *My marriage is showing some strain because I can't stop talking about it. I am also afraid that my daughters will think that I am weak.*

DREW: *Do you want to transfer to another facility?*

ESTHER: *I am afraid that Emily would give me a bad recommendation. I know that department heads usually support each other and I would not be able to explain Emily's negativity toward me to another potential supervisor.*

STAGE FOUR BETWEEN DREW THOMPSON AND FOOD SERVICES EMPLOYEE ESTHER CABRERA

After Stage One and hearing the employee's perspective, the facilitator next focuses on Stage Four, Problem Solving. A proven technique for helping the employee think through the situation clearly is by *reality testing*. Asking these types of questions helps the employee see the options as clearly as possible and helps the employee make the decision that is best for him or her. The goal in this stage is to honestly explore what options are available and then to help the employee think through the consequences—good and bad—of each possible option. One key element of asking reality testing questions is to do so in a way that does not seem to put the employee in the "hot seat" or to "grill" the employee in a negative way. The questions are asked not to interrogate but instead to assist the employee in thinking through his or her options in a reflective, supportive way. The tone of the questions (reflective), the pace of asking them (slowly, thoughtfully), and the attitude of the person meeting with the employee (open, supportive) all matter. Here are some things to keep in mind:

▶ What realistic alternatives does the employee have?

▶ Can he or she transfer to another department?

▶ If the employee can make a transfer, what does the employee know about the new workplace?

▶ Has he or she spoken with employees in the new workplace to ascertain that it would be a more supportive atmosphere than the current one, and not just a move from one bad workplace to another?

► What would be the process of initiating a transfer to another department, if it is possible?

► How would the employee handle the time in the current job before the transfer actually occurred?

► If the employee were to transfer, how would his or her coworkers view his or her leaving?

► Would the employee be viewed as someone who abandoned his or her job or as a hero or heroine?

► If the employee decides to seek employment elsewhere, does he or she have any leads?

► Who does the employee know who might be able to help? One can negotiate better with a job offer pending than with only a plan to read the want ads online or in the newspaper.

► Could the employee manage financially if he or she left and another job did not materialize?

► Will the employee's mental or physical health be affected if the employee decides to stay?

Esther probably could not transfer to another department. There were no openings in the clinic minicafeteria. While Esther seemed to be Emily's chief victim, other employees also dreaded coming to work and feared that they might be next. It was a toxic environment. Esther realized that she might have to consider working in fast food for a while or even move her family to an area where another hospital was hiring food service workers. Esther had not investigated what unemployment would mean to her. While her husband had a job as a school facilities coordinator, the family needed her income.

Esther realized that she had been so stressed that her family and her health were already affected. She decided that she would talk with her family, that she would begin looking for another job, perhaps even a different type of job, and that she would say nothing to Emily until she had found another job.

Drew promised confidentiality, as he would have done in a more traditional Exchange process. Just making a decision was a relief for Esther. Her posture straightened and she held her head up as she left Drew's office. Drew's job was not to make a decision for Esther, but rather to help her make the best decision for herself, based on the best information available. Esther's decision allowed her to assert control over her life and leave with a realistic hope for something better, as well as a plan for finding it.

Using The Exchange with the Bully Boss

So what about Emily Smith and other bully bosses? Unless you are the direct supervisor of the bully boss with power over his or her job and paycheck, these are indeed difficult people to deal with. It may be necessary to meet with Emily separately, in an adaptation to the process for disruptive employees (see Chapter 8) if the situation that Esther is encountering proves to be a pattern of behavior. If Emily's superior does need to have that meeting with her, Esther's information that she has shared in her discussion with Drew would need to remain confidential from Emily.

Sometimes bully bosses respond to offers of "advanced" training where topics about the benefits of good worker morale are on the agenda. Emily, for example, was hoping for a promotion to administration and welcomed any opportunity to advance herself. She had achieved her current status almost by accident (the previous director had died of a heart attack) and had not received specific training in supervising. If such training includes other directors, bully bosses can sometimes hear advice coming from peers that they are not able to hear from employees or even from superiors. In the first case, they assume the employees don't know what they are talking about; in the latter case, they assume they are being criticized and go into defensive mode and are unable to hear constructive suggestions. In training, the collective wisdom and leadership of a group of skilled healthcare managers often creates the positive peer pressure that bully bosses need, especially when they have gotten other feedback from their managers. In the end, the potential damage to morale, employee retention and satisfaction, and patient safety issues because of a lack of good communication skills all indicate that it is in the best interest of the healthcare facility to manage bully bosses. The Exchange process and techniques can aid in managing this situation successfully.

11

Using The Exchange Techniques with Patients

As Radha Samson was making her way to meet with Dr. Garcia about his staff problems, she passed the new long-term care building and remembered one of her first experiences with The Exchange. It was two years ago, during the final stages of the building's construction, when everyone was stressed with the noise and delays. She had been contacted by the Vice President (VP) of Ambulatory Services, Dr. Gunther Samuels, about an issue that had come up between Nursing Duty Night Supervisor Kim Brown and a patient, Marvin Yee. Dr. Samuels was new to St. Sonia's Hospital and had called Radha for advice. His concern was that Mr. Yee was one of St. Sonia's Hospital's major financial contributors and Kim Brown was one of the most important members of his staff. It pleased Radha to think of how well the situation had worked out. This was the same Kim Brown, now a trained Exchange facilitator herself and promoted to a new position as well, who had just used The Exchange that very day.

USING THE EXCHANGE TO DEAL WITH PATIENT EXPECTATIONS OF HOSPITAL STAFF

To deal with the conflict between Mr. Yee and Kim Brown, Radha first spoke with Dr. Samuels and then decided to try out The Exchange. It seemed like a perfect opportunity: the issues, she had heard, showed that there was a misunderstanding and the patient's expectations about the role of hospital staff were unmet. She remembered being happy that it would also be a good opportunity for Marvin Yee, as both a patient and a donor, to find out how The Exchange actually worked.

The situation involved Mr. Yee's request for a room transfer. He had been in the hospital for over a month with complications following abdominal surgery. He had not asked for special treatment and had had several roommates during his stay in the outmoded long-term care wing. He was keenly aware that the new building, when finished, would prevent other patients from having to endure the overcrowding that prevented him from having a private room and forcing him now to share space with an "impossible" roommate. But he felt that his "understandable" request for a room transfer was being *deliberately* ignored. He was convinced that the roommate was suffering from dementia because he spent a lot of time arguing loudly with someone who wasn't there. Mr. Yee knew that Dr. Samuels had endorsed his room change request, so he wondered why the nurses hadn't moved him by now. He was exhausted from a lack of sleep and he was angry. He wanted to be *acknowledged*.

STAGE ONE: RADHA SAMSON'S PRIVATE MEETINGS WITH PATIENT MARVIN YEE AND NURSING DUTY NIGHT SUPERVISOR KIM BROWN

In her first conversation with him, Radha learned that Mr. Yee had great respect for Dr. Samuels but felt that the nursing duty night supervisor Kim Brown was not doing her job. He felt that she seemed oblivious to what was happening with his roommate situation, despite the room change request he submitted a day earlier. He had said that he didn't want special treatment, but he also didn't want to be ignored. He complained that no one should have to make eight calls; one should have been enough!

When she spoke to Kim, Radha found another exhausted person. The disruption caused by the construction, the constraints of the current facility, and the frustration of an unusually large patient load were taking a toll on Kim. Under normal circumstances, the room change request would have been easily accommodated, but that day there had been 15 admissions and Kim did not even have beds for the eight who had been admitted during the evening; three were being held in the emergency room (ER) and five were being held in the postanesthesia care unit (PACU). Further, she had no idea that the complaining patient was an important hospital donor. She only knew that he had been paging her every half hour since she came on duty.

Radha remembered that Mr. Yee did finally get his room changed. Though he remained disgruntled, he agreed to a meeting, which he called a "confrontation," with "that nurse."

STAGE THREE: RADHA SAMSON'S JOINT MEETING WITH PATIENT MARVIN YEE AND NURSING DUTY NIGHT SUPERVISOR KIM BROWN

The joint meeting between Marvin Yee and Kim Brown began with an apology from Kim to Mr. Yee and an explanation of what had been on her plate when the problem began. Then Mr. Yee tendered his own apology to Kim for his annoying, insistent paging.

During the joint meeting, Radha, Kim, and Mr. Yee had talked together about how to make future communications easier between nurses and patients. Since then, a new intercom system has been installed that allows patients to immediately communicate their needs to staff, who could then acknowledge the patients' request and give an approximate time when nurses would be able to come and give assistance.

In addition, as a result of the joint meeting, St. Sonia's Hospital instituted a patient ombuds program, which requires that all ombuds be trained in The Exchange process. It was, in fact, a donation from Mr. Yee that made this possible.

St. Sonia's Hospital's policies now require and support staff at all levels to make it a priority to solicit and handle patient concerns. The Exchange provides an informal process for looking at whatever systemic issues were involved or with any situation that could not be resolved with a simple conversation on the spot. This policy of encouraging patients to talk about their concerns as they arose, and before making a formal complaint, has proved to be a big success. Not only have fewer formal complaints or lawsuits been initiated, but it is clear from patient satisfaction surveys that such an approach is most welcome.

USING THE EXCHANGE TO DEAL WITH MEDICAL ERROR

Obviously, The Exchange is not the right mechanism for addressing every patient or staff complaint, but it can be used to deal with a wide variety of problems—even with medical error. Studies of medical mistakes indicate that most patients have the same interests. What they typically want is:

▶ An acknowledgment that a problem occurred

▶ An apology

▶ Redress of their grievances—having their expenses covered, for instance

▶ Assurance that the same thing won't happen to another patient, perhaps through a change in policy It comes as no surprise to any human resources person that these are the very same things that dedicated employees also want. So how might an administrator, a patient relations representative, or an ombuds approach the possibility of convening The Exchange when a patient believes that medical error has occurred and a staff member is involved?

Sometimes the patient is contacted first by the ombuds or patient relations representative and presented with the opportunity to voice his or her complaint directly to the "offending" provider. It is probably preferable, though, when the staff member is a high-level employee to make sure that that person is on board before the patient is invited to participate. Should the patient agree first but then the staff member prove unwilling, it could escalate the conflict and the patient might feel it was the entire institution that let him or her down. There are countless stories of lawsuits against medical facilities with one of the issues being that the patient never had the chance to directly address the person perceived to have caused the problem. Instead, complaints got diverted through the bureaucracy and the patient felt dismissed and lost in red tape.

Consider the case of Paula McGregor. Paula believed that the hysterectomy she was subjected to had turned out to be unnecessary.

During a periodic checkup for endometriosis, her gynecologist recommended a biopsy that revealed complex hyperplasia with atypia. An ultrasound showed thickening of the uterus and, as was the standard of care at the time, she was given a total hysterectomy.

Following the surgery, the tissue was examined by a pathologist who found no signs of disease. The pathologist informed Paula's primary physician of the results, who in turn disclosed the findings to Paula. Paula was devastated and felt furious. Unable to speak directly to her surgeon, Dr. Ivan Petraeus, to discuss what had happened, Paula felt stonewalled and began to wonder about the doctor's competence. Did he have a pattern of misread biopsies? She consulted an attorney about filing a lawsuit.

The ombuds at St Sonia's was able to persuade both Dr. Petraeus and the patient herself to participate in an Exchange. Paula was assured that her participation did not preclude further action, and with her attorney's support, she decided to try it.

STAGE THREE: JOINT MEETING BETWEEN PATIENT PAULA McGREGOR AND SURGEON DR. IVAN PETRAEUS

The chance to speak directly to Dr. Ivan Petraeus, the provider she held responsible for her hysterectomy came as a relief to Paula McGregor. She was able to ask questions about how the recommendation to perform the surgery had been made. She wanted to know about the doctor's past experience with hysterectomies. Then she was also able to hear how the situation had affected the doctor—he was haunted by the biopsy but felt that he had done the right thing, based on the information he had at the time. Each could see the other as a human being affected by a common experience. Paula's husband was a doctor and she was not interested in making money off the situation; she just wanted to be treated respectfully.

Once Paula understood that Dr. Petraeus was neither incompetent nor inexperienced, she was willing to think about ways that other women could be spared her experience. She agreed to take the lead in forming a volunteer task force of women who had undergone gynecological surgery. Paula would offer to meet with women scheduled for similar interventions to hear their worries and concerns, and to talk to them about what they might expect. Dr. Petraeus volunteered to help the women of the task force learn more about his department and assist them in developing the information to share with future patients.

Journalist and author Malcolm Gladwell notes in his best-selling book *Blink: The Power of Thinking Without Thinking* (Boston: Little Brown/Back Bay Books, 2005, p. 40):

> *The risk of being sued for malpractice has very little to do with how many mistakes a doctor makes. Analyses of malpractice lawsuits show that there are highly skilled doctors who get sued a lot and doctors who make lots of mistakes and never get sued . . . patients don't file lawsuits because they've been harmed by shoddy medical care and* something else *happens to them. The something else is how they were treated, on a personal level by their doctor.*

Mistakes, errors of judgment, or whatever may give a patient concern are not necessarily "shoddy" treatment but may be interpreted as such if not addressed. Our experience is that most patients can understand and accept mistakes or lapses in the quality of care as long as their concerns about a negative experience are acknowledged and any consequences addressed. The Exchange provides an opportunity to do this.

Marvin Yee and Paula McGregor were not looking for monetary compensation from St. Sonia's. But they did want to understand what had happened and why. And they wanted to hear it directly from the person that they felt had injured them. Most importantly, they wanted to be part of a solution.

In the following chapter, we examine how The Exchange can be used with the patients and their families.

CHAPTER 12

The Exchange and Patients' Families

In every workplace, including hospitals, conflicts can include parties who are not present. We call them *shadow participants*, but in reality they may be much more substantial than mere shadows. When patients are involved, either as principals or as subjects of disputes, these shadow participants may be more powerful than the patients. The shadow participants become *surrogate voices* for the ones they love or support. They are the families: the spouses, partners, children, parents, and relatives whose lives are affected by whatever the patients are experiencing. When patients are not able to speak for themselves, and often even when they are, the surrogate or shadow parties can be invited to participate in a Dispute Resolution process. Sometimes they have legal standing, such as a Power of Attorney for Healthcare, and sometimes they don't, but they are related to patients and believe they speak for them. Whether or not families are active participants, they are affected by the patients' treatment; therefore, taking the interests of family members into account is critical to a successful Exchange process.

THE ADVANTAGES OF USING THE EXCHANGE TECHNIQUES WITH PATIENTS' FAMILIES

Cases involving decision making by family members about patient care are never easy. They involve high emotions. Yet the opportunity to speak in a structured process monitored by the facilitators allows the parties in the situation to express those emotions and be heard in a respectful way and then to think more rationally during the decision-making process.

In the private meeting (Stage One), the facilitator may need to help the family member consider his or her choice of words, tone, and fundamental interests. The facilitator helps one family member decide if the purpose of his or her action is to prove that the other family member is wrong or is to do what is best for their loved one. The facilitator can help one family member find language that won't cause the other family member to tune out.

Without the structure of The Exchange's Stage Three—attention to an *icebreaker*, the *impact*, and the *issues*—it would be very difficult to move beyond blame and self-righteous declarations. In times of emotional stress, human brains (and the human beings whose skulls they inhabit) are flooded with emotion-producing chemicals that make it difficult to think logically and participate in more dispassionate discussion. Having a facilitator to keep the process moving forward allows an empathic exchange of feelings and a constructive conversation about alternatives.

The facilitator may assume the role of coach in situations among family members or between patients and their families, just as he or she coaches the provider in a provider-patient case. The facilitator is often dealing with vulnerable individuals, consumed with their own perspective of the situation.

However, people cannot just "set aside" their emotions. During the joint meeting (Stage Three) the facilitator may need to be alert to the need for intervening as soon as the conversation seems to veer off into blame or unproductive anger. The facilitator plays a balancing role in these conflicts; his or her role is not to defend either party but to help each party to explain him- or herself to the other in ways that can be heard.

THE EXCHANGE BETWEEN A PROVIDER AND A PATIENT'S PARENT

Along with the Patient Relations staff, Radha Samson has had experience with patients' families. Radha was about 10 minutes early as she arrived at the cafeteria for her meeting with St. Sonia's lab director, Dr.

Raul Garcia. She was pouring herself a cup of coffee when she felt a tap on her shoulder. Radha turned to find Tanya Stewart, a nurse practitioner she had met about 10 months ago during a hastily scheduled meeting in the Patient Relations Department. Tanya was there to respond to a complaint made by the father of a young patient. Radha didn't remember much about the meeting except that Tanya had been thinking about handing in her resignation. Radha did recall that the meeting ended with her suggestion to invite the patient's father to an Exchange meeting that would be facilitated by a representative of the Patient Relations Department. She also remembered learning from the subsequent report that a successful process had been accomplished.

Before Radha could even say hello, Tanya said, *"Just want to tell you that you saved my career!"* A little taken aback, and curious too, Radha set down her coffee and invited Tanya to join her and share her experience. *"Tell me about it,"* she said. Then she waited. Tanya quickly filled her in:

You may not remember the situation. It was a father complaining that I had misdiagnosed his son's serious ear infection when he had come in to ask for antibiotics. Actually, he demanded antibiotics, and I tried to make him understand that at that moment, it was not the appropriate treatment. While the boy—he was three years old—did have a low-grade fever and loss of appetite and lethargy, his nasal passages were clear, his throat showed no erythema or edema, and the tympanic membranes were clear; all his symptoms were consistent with the flu. And it was the flu season. I recommended fluids and rest along with Tylenol to reduce the fever. I could tell the father was not happy but I'd done the standard workup, the clinic was crowded with others with more serious symptoms, and I TRIED to explain that antibiotics, if not needed, could cause resistant bacteria to develop and in the long term hinder his son's ability to resist infection. Well, 18 hours later the father brought his son to the ER and the staff there diagnosed an ear infection. The boy was treated but the father was furious and the next day he stormed into Patient Relations to file a complaint about my neglect.

Radha nodded empathetically as a signal to the young woman to continue.

Tanya continued:

I was devastated because I thought I had been so clear and compassionate in our first meeting when I tried to explain what was likely happening to the boy. I had always wanted to work in pediatrics and until this situation I believed I was on my way to the career I wanted. But I started to question not only my skills but my "calling" too. I remember you suggested that the dad be invited to participate in an Exchange process. To my surprise, he agreed.

Radha asked Tanya to continue.
Tanya continued:

Well, we talked through the whole thing with the help of Betsy Rose from Patient Relations. [Stage Three] The dad was really angry at the beginning and I was defensive about my diagnosis—which I still think was reasonable given what I knew then— but I learned that this kid had a history of ear infections that I hadn't known about and that the father, who was a single dad, saw the familiar symptoms developing and was frantic that no one seemed to be listening to him. Anyway, I'm back on track with my career! And I think the dad learned some new things about ear infections and about antibiotics and what a nurse practitioner does.

In this example, Tanya was a hospital staff member. The issue was the appropriateness of her behavior as a provider.

THE IMPORTANCE OF STAGE ONE OF THE EXCHANGE WITH THE FAMILIES OF PATIENTS

Stage One is extremely important in cases that include patients and their families. It is often important for the patient and his or her family to know that the hospital staff has *heard* them and *understands* their situation. Feeling heard can help them move forward. The Patient Relations staff person who is facilitating The Exchange meets first with the patient and/or the family to get a sense of what happened and what the concerns are.

The facilitator may need to make a judgment call about planning a joint meeting for the patient and the family with the provider. It is best not to offer such a meeting until the Patient Relations staff person has a chance to meet with the provider and assess the situation. One Patient Relations employee who utilizes The Exchange methodology on an ongoing basis with the issues that she manages shared with us that she tells patients and their families at the end of Stage One that she will:

▶ Look into the issues.

▶ Talk to the provider.

▶ Be sure to *get back to them as soon as she can.*

This gives her the wiggle room to decide if the best option is to bring in the provider (her first choice) or for her to assist the patient's family in another way. The Stage One meeting that the facilitator holds with the provider is important as well. Having a chance to air his or her frustrations about the situation without being judged can be very helpful for the provider of care.

Besides hearing the provider's perspective, the Patient Relations staff can use Stage One meetings to coach providers. At these sessions, facilitators can give providers tips about listening and talking to patients and their families in a way that acknowledges their pain, and tips about not sounding defensive.

THE USE OF STAGES THREE AND FOUR OF THE EXCHANGE WITH THE FAMILIES OF PATIENTS

If there is a Stage Three of The Exchange for patients and their families to meet together with the provider, it is still planned around the classic discussions of the *icebreaker, impact,* and *issues.* As the facilitator prepares for Stage Three, he or she considers the reality that discussing the impact can be somewhat challenging in these Patient Relations Department cases because of the inherent imbalance in the situation.

The goal would be to give more time to the patient and/or family so that they feel fully heard. Although the emphasis would need to be on the personal reactions of the patient and the family, the provider might be asked to discuss his or her feelings regarding:

▶ Frustration about the patient's self-care when there has been noncompliance

▶ Regret and disappointment when there has been an occurrence of medical error

▶ Hopes for a resolution when there has been a systemwide problem

Allowing providers to vent in Stage One, offering coaching, and a careful explanation of the plan for the joint meeting helps providers focus on the patient/family group when they all talk together in Stage Three.

Stage Four of the process can be quite concrete. In these types of cases, it is not unusual for one outcome to be an improvement in the way a procedure is managed, so that the medical error or lack of communication by hospital staff does not occur again. Many patients and their families are looking not only to be heard, they also desire to ensure that others do not experience the same type of situation. Stage Four affords the parties the opportunity to explore how that might be accomplished.

THE EXCHANGE INVOLVING TWO FAMILY MEMBERS AS SHADOW PARTICIPANTS

In other situations, the Patient Relations Department can facilitate The Exchange between two family members. What follows is an example of that type of process.

The patient was a 32-year-old man who had been severely injured in a motorcycle accident and was in a persistent vegetative state. He was being kept alive by machines. In the absence of a document giving anyone power of attorney for his medical decisions, the attending physician had asked the man's wife if she wished to continue treatment. The young man's mother was also present for the discussion and clearly believed she had the right to make the decision, or at least have her opinion be given significant weight. The dispute was between the two relatives—the man's wife and the man's mother—who disagreed over what to do. The hospital's Ethics Committee had agreed to support whatever decision the family made, but wanted the decision to be acceptable to the whole family.

The mother, a deeply religious woman, believed that only God should decide when a person died and therefore that her beloved son should be kept alive by any means possible. She hinted that her daughter-in-law wanted her son to die so that she could get money from his life-insurance policy to pay bills the couple had accrued.

The daughter-in-law wanted to do what she thought her active, sports-loving husband would have wanted. They did not have a "living will," which would have made his wishes clear. They had talked about creating one but just hadn't gotten around to it. Still, she knew he would not want to continue to live "without a life." She implied that her mother-in-law was an interfering and judgmental person who had made marriage to her son complicated.

Both women loved the young man and had a deep emotional involvement in the question of how to proceed. When the idea of a facilitated Exchange process was raised, both agreed. In this case, the facilitator's interests were to respect the relatives' wishes and to assist in the communication in a way that helped the family move forward.

After brief separate meetings with the patient's mother and patient's wife (Stage One), the facilitator (part of the Exchange team at the Patient Relations Department) began Stage Three with a topic that allowed both women to talk about the young man, and each began to appreciate the depth of love that the other had for him.

The facilitator then moved to the issue of how this situation was affecting each of them. They had a first-in-a-lifetime opportunity to talk together about the development of their personal values and how these affected their current thinking. They were able to examine their own interests (what was most important to each of them) and to think about what the patient himself might have wanted.

As they moved in and out of Stage Four, Problem Solving, the two women began *together* to develop a strategy for making a decision that would honor the young man's values, apart from either of theirs. They decided to remove the young man from the machines, and he passed away 18 hours later with his wife and his mother at his side.

It takes courage for individuals to agree to participate in The Exchange process in a hospital. They may perceive that they are playing on unfair turf—the healthcare institution where the loved one is being housed. They may fear that their own reputation is at risk with other "shadow" constituents, other family members who may not be physically present but who will demand answers and possibly blame them for incorrect decisions. They may feel that to participate in a discussion would be counter to the norm of sticking up for one's own point of view.

The rewards of participating in The Exchange process, however, are great! The possibilities of moving on with one's life or achieving closure at a painful time are not insignificant gifts. Too many people carry around for years the real or perceived injuries they have received at the hands of another. The consequences of opportunities lost because of being preoccupied this way and the reality of being stuck in pain are serious. The Exchange process provides a respectful, helpful way to begin the future.

13

Using The Exchange in Group Conflicts

Out of the corner of her eye, Radha Samson saw Dr. Raul Garcia, the director of St. Sonia's lab, coming in the door of the cafeteria and rose to meet him. Tanya Stewart, the nurse practitioner with whom Radha had been chatting, noticed the situation and tactfully took her cup of coffee to another table.

Dr. Garcia headed up the laboratories that had responsibility for all of St. Sonia's Hospital. Dr. Garcia met Radha's glance and seemed to relax almost immediately. He pointed to a corner table where they could talk privately, and she joined him there. Dr. Garcia told Radha:

I need an iced tea, but it'll just take a minute. I want to pick your brain about how to handle some issues that have little to do with what we do professionally but everything to do with how other people think we should be doing things. I'm afraid we're going to have a wholesale mutiny in my staff if we don't do something quickly.

As they talked, Radha realized there were several key issues, as well as some tangential ones:

1. Requests from certain departments (mainly Internal Medicine and Ear, Nose, and Throat (ENT) were accompanied by written demands for unrealistic turnaround times; then complaints came in when these deadlines couldn't be met.

2. Some physicians were having their assistants make lab requests by phone, bypassing the new computer system, and a few of

those orders had been dropped because of a misunderstanding about how to enter them.

3. Lab technicians were feeling overworked and undervalued due to the sheer volume of requests during the current flu season.

4. Phone and front-desk coverage during lunch and afternoon breaks (mandatory per the bargaining contract) was spread thin due to budgetary constraints; other departments that had promised backup coverage were often unresponsive or had no one to spare. Research technicians were pitching in, but morale was beginning to suffer.

Radha knew that Dr. Garcia was a good supervisor, and she wanted him to feel supported in his efforts to boost morale for his hardworking crew. As they talked, it became apparent that the department was a very tightly knit team and that losing any one staff person would probably result in the loss of several more people. She also realized that there were hospitals in the region that might be glad to hire from this highly respected group. They would be very hard to replace. Radha proposed:

Why not have a facilitated Exchange discussion with the team? We need to have everyone involved. And we need to develop better protocols for communicating with other departments. I could get Drew Johnson to facilitate the meeting. And if you can get coverage that fast, we could do it the day after tomorrow at noon. Drew reserves that time for situations just like this. We can have lunch brought in so that no one needs to miss a meal.

PLANNING AND CONDUCTING THE EXCHANGE WITH A GROUP OF LAB EMPLOYEES AND THEIR DIRECTOR

So how might Employee Relations Director Drew Johnson conduct an Exchange meeting with a highly opinionated and competent group of 15 employees and their director—and cover everything in only one hour? Radha would fill him in on what she had learned and he would need to talk with Dr. Raul Garcia himself (Stage One) prior to any meeting with his staff, but Drew probably would not have to talk to each member of the department. However, he could check in with some long-term staff to get a sense of the issues from the lab employees' perspectives. He could also anticipate that a follow-up meeting might be required for an assessment of what had been resolved successfully in the first session and where effort was still needed.

It would be important to spend some time designing a Stage Two agenda for the group meeting. With only one hour to address multiple issues among the 16 employees in the lab, the meeting itself would have to be conducted expeditiously.

Drew realized immediately that the issues underlying the "conflicts" were both internal and external, which needed to be analyzed first. The external issues relating to interactions with other departments were more pressing; the first step might be to devise a strategic plan to consider these, rather than opening discussions with other departments. Nonetheless, there would have to be interdepartmental meetings if any strategy were to work. Those meetings could be scheduled once the department group had agreed on the best approach.

Drew considered that after meeting with the group, he might decide to table the front-desk coverage issue and handle it separately with the four staff members who were most affected. Or that issue could be discussed as part of the larger issue of how to meet "outside-the-department" demands, which were proving so difficult to accommodate with the current staff. The important concern would be to include everyone in the discussion and not let anyone dominate the conversation.

USING THE EXCHANGE TO RESOLVE ISSUES BETWEEN TWO SEPARATE DEPARTMENTS

There are times when a facilitator is asked to work with two separate departments to resolve an issue between them. The departments involved here are the Intensive Care Unit (ICU) and the Hospice unit.

An elderly man who had been brought into the ICU with a suspected heart attack had been placed on life-support systems that included an intravenous (IV) and other equipment and monitors which were attached to his bed as well as to his arms. Family members held his hand and watched anxiously as he appeared to be failing—no eye movement, no brain movement on the monitor, just labored and painful breathing. They eventually decided to honor his written wishes and asked hospital staff to remove life support. The ICU staff agreed to move him to the nearby Hospice unit of the hospital. Trailing IVs, the whole family moved with the old man's gurney to the Hospice area and continued their vigil with the support of the Hospice staff.

With no warning, the door to the Hospice room was thrown open and two nurses from the ICU burst in and moved toward the bed. One of the nurses blurted out:

> *Why are you using our equipment? We can barely keep up. You have your own stuff. Look at this. The IV clearly says, ICU.*

The tension in the room left the family unsettled about the care at the hospital. When "Grandma" showed distress and later said to the family, *"How can they focus on my husband when they are fighting like this?"* her grown granddaughter lodged a complaint at the hospital. Now two issues had to be dealt with: the issues between the hospital and the family (which the Patient Relations staff managed with just a Stage One conversation, allowing family members to vent) *and* helping the two departments work through the issues between them. The stunned family watched as the Hospice staff tried to respond.

THE EXCHANGE, STAGE ONE:
THE PRIVATE GROUP MEETINGS

Radha Samson facilitated The Exchange process to deal with the issues between the Hospice and ICU staffs. In Stage One, she met with all members of one department and then the other to hear their litany of frustrations with their colleagues. She asked each group to select three representatives—individuals who were trusted and had good communication skills.

While most Exchange meetings are held with the primary parties, a departmental conflict will work best with group representatives who can see the bigger picture, one beyond their own department. Note that

Radha did not choose the representatives. She did suggest criteria for their selection, but she left the choice to the department members.

The Exchange, Stage Two: Developing the Group Agenda

In her agenda planning (Stage Two), Radha added the issue that had not been specifically raised in the separate meetings: *how the incident had affected the patient's family and, by extension, the reputation of St. Sonia's Hospital.* A Patient Relations representative had spent time with the family, which was grieving over the death of the grandfather and did not wish to participate in another meeting, but they asked Radha to convey their shock and disappointment to the staff over what had happened.

The Exchange, Stage Three: The Joint Meeting of the Groups

When working with groups, here are some suggestions for facilitating the joint meeting of Stage Three that will help accomplish the goals of both the administration—Director of Employee Relations Drew Thompson, Lab Director Dr. Raul Garcia, and Radha Sampson—and the staffs of the Hospice and the ICU.

Don't forsake the strategy:

▸ Present the *icebreaker.*

▸ Recognize the *impact* or emotional toll that the situation is having on the groups.

▸ Discuss the *issues* affecting the groups.

▸ Move on to *problem solving*, but not too quickly.

ICEBREAKER

In group settings, participants need time to buy into the process before they can participate in it productively. Having the chance to speak at the beginning of the meeting—especially in response to an *icebreaker* that elicits positive feelings and answers—gives participants a stake in the session.

Of course with everyone's time at a premium, the buy-in time needs to be limited and handled efficiently. One way to accomplish this is to set an arbitrary time (for example, 30 seconds) or word limit (for example, five words or less) for each speaker in turn, which will encourage those who are shy to share information and make it harder for the more talkative individuals to dominate the discussion. A time or word limit makes it fair for everyone.

If you are working with individuals who are all part of one department or team, a good *icebreaker* would be a question that reminds the group of their "good times" or joint accomplishments, or asks about their original inspiration or personal commitment. But you do have to explain why you are starting this way. For example, you might begin by saying something like this:

> *Before we get to the "meat" of this meeting, we have found that it is very helpful to begin with a reminder of the big picture—of why you are all here at St. Sonia's. So please tell us in five words or less what you like best about your job.*

If you are working with two departments, you might want to start with something less personal: have each person say his or her name and role in the department. Many times people who work in the same institution don't know what colleagues in different departments really do. Learning and using names instead of titles goes a long way toward leveling the playing field between groups who know each other only by reputation. Nametags or table tents can be helpful, too.

You will find the tension level in the room going down after the first three or four speakers take their turns. The *icebreaker* gives everyone a chance to relax before dealing with the issues that divide them. Don't sound too serious as you go through this step. Remember how important your tone is; much of what people remember from an experience is the tone. You will discover that, most often, people adjust their tone to match yours. If you hear only variations of the same theme, change the topic midway. For example:

Okay, it's clear, most of you like your jobs. Now tell us why the rest of the hospital needs you so much. And again you have a five-word limit.

As in other uses of The Exchange, the facilitator here is participating as a stakeholder and can model what is wanted from the others. In managing group conflicts, some facilitators like to capture these brief positive responses to the icebreaker on a large flip chart. They remain visible as a subtle reminder that there are good things about working at the institution should the discussion bog down in complaints about what is wrong.

IMPACT

As you move from the *icebreaker* to the *impact*, you might consider a new approach. By now most participants will have bought into the process and feel ready to move forward. This time, ask for someone (choose a volunteer, or pick someone if you think no one might volunteer) to talk about how the situation is affecting them. Then you might ask the group:

Is this how all of you feel? If not, does someone have another experience to add?

You should limit this topic to prevent it from devolving into a complaining session when the real goal here is to find solutions. Then treat a similar topic in the same way. One person begins and the rest add details as they come to mind during the discussion.

How is this affecting the work of the department?

Note here that the first impact question allows some venting on a *personal* level, and the second impact question helps the group to focus briefly on the effect in the department.

The Exchange, Stage Four: Problem Solving by the Groups

Then, it's time to begin problem solving. Issue by issue, the movement into Stage Four is not rushed but not belabored. As in the classic model of The Exchange:

▸ Define

▸ Determine

▸ Develop

▸ Decide

▸ Document

Radha made sure that those selected by each group to take part in Stage Four would have the trust of their coworkers and the authority to make decisions on their behalf. She also made sure that those from the departments who were not attending the meeting knew that their representatives would let them know what transpired.

A variation on the classic problem solving of Stage Four is to divide the group by the number of issues to be resolved. Try to make sure that each group is made up of individuals who represent a variety of perspectives. Each group is assigned a different issue to process, which they are asked to define and develop, and then make tentative recommendations for solving. After a brief time, 10 minutes or so, the groups report their conclusions and recommendations to everyone; all of the participants can contribute additional suggestions. Surprisingly, even when there has been tension within a working group, there is often great progress with this small-group method of problem solving.

Drew might divide the lab team of 15 employees plus Dr. Garcia into four problem-solving groups. Each group could be assigned a topic. For example, the four individuals affected by the issue involving front-desk coverage could be the ones to brainstorm that issue.

It is important that before the end of the session the whole group hears from each subgroup. After each report, the larger group is invited to add to the list of recommendations. The idea is that whatever resolution is reached will belong to everyone, not just the group that proposed it. Sometimes, as with the ICU and Hospice departments, final decisions may be delayed for a day or two to give people a chance for further informal discussion or to report back to their fellow workers. But it is important that decisions be made quickly so that everyone can get back to their primary work.

Working with groups provides slightly different challenges than working with two individuals, but many facilitators find it more interesting and even fun. Additional personalities add energy and contribute more ideas. In the end, group decisions usually have a wider effect and the reputation of The Exchange is enhanced as more people talk about how useful it was.

PART FOUR | **Beyond The Workplace**

Using The Exchange Techniques on Yourself

Radha Samson got back to her office, looked at her watch, and realized that by delaying her departure another 45 minutes, she would avoid much of the homebound traffic. Instead of leaving right then, she would go and work out at the gym in the Sub-Acute Care Facility attached to the new building. This would accomplish several goals. Radha would get:

- ▶ The chance to see the new back machines that had just been installed at the request of staff physical therapists.

- ▶ The opportunity to do real exercise beyond walking from building to building; she needed to build up strength for the upcoming citywide 5K race in which the hospital was fielding a team.

- ▶ The opportunity to take a mental break from her daily schedule.

- ▶ The chance to think about what she was going to say to her son, Anan, about the car when she got home for dinner; earlier that day he had sent excited text messages about "needing" it to drive to Disneyland, with friends she assumed, and she did not like the thought of it at all.

Radha pulled her gym bag from the bottom drawer of her desk and sat back for a moment to text to her son, Anan:

Be home in an hour, w/ pizza. Don't forget to feed the dog.
Talk then.

Then she grabbed her bag and headed for the gym. Radha was following her self-prescribed plan to avoid burnout.

Medical professionals are often attracted to their careers because of early personal experiences. Radha, for example, had wanted to become a doctor ever since she had watched her grandmother die a painful death from lung cancer. When she was growing up, her grandmother lived with her family, so Radha had watched the sincere but eventually futile efforts of care providers to help her grandmother breathe with less difficulty. Also, she had seen the desperate efforts of the doctors when she was eventually hospitalized. Kim Brown became a nurse because of family tradition in the healthcare field. Drew Thompson's younger brother had died of cystic fibrosis. The examples are many. The result is legions of extremely dedicated and hardworking care providers who are highly motivated to make health care better for patients and providers.

The downside, as many readers will recognize, is that along with the passion to make a difference comes a tendency to become so involved in the practice of "doing good" that you lose track of your own needs. As a result, you may harbor a judgmental attitude toward anyone who doesn't share your drive and tendency to overwork. It may also lead to mental and/or physical exhaustion. Then, of course, you are no good to anyone, including your family and friends; these are your *shadow participants* that we spoke about in Chapter 12 who are affected by conflicts and the issues that you face. So what should you do?

Well, let's look at how using The Exchange on yourself might work and could help you avoid burnout and exhaustion, and the mistakes that often result. Start with the nonjudgmental tone that a facilitator maintains. No one is harder on themselves than healthcare workers, for whom mistakes can be deadly and who live by the motto, "Do no harm." As we have seen, the nonjudgmental attitude used by the facilitator with employees in The Exchange helps those employees take responsibility for whatever happened in a less defensive way and makes forward movement possible. It can also help you look more objectively at your own needs or miscalculations.

A sense that making a mistake equates with personal failure leads many people to deny or cover up the normal mistakes we all make. Even worse is the climate of dishonesty that ensues; if one is not comfortable admitting a mistake, then mistakes are nonexistent and they can't be addressed or corrected.

So the first step in addressing burnout (or its early warning signs) is to accept your own humanity and the chance that you are likely, at some point, to make a few mistakes and that is okay. It may take some practice but it will be a big step in self-care to view your mistakes as *information about something that did not work*—and therefore can be avoided in the future—rather than as something that is insupportable or unforgivable. Such an attitude allows you to share the information, as appropriate, with those affected and figure out ways to deal with the fallout or to avoid making the same mistake again. Interestingly, encouraging such an attitude in the workplace makes it more likely that big mistakes will be avoided by others because people will feel more comfortable talking to each other—discussing innovations more openly perhaps—and become increasingly able to take comments as suggestions rather than as criticism.

Be willing to talk about a mistake you made that led to serious consequences. Don't talk about the mistake to everyone, as talking too much may indeed undermine your reputation. But talk to whomever was affected.

As appropriate, bring up the occasional mistakes that you have made. Doing so will help others deal with their mistakes. It's comforting to know that even higher-ups can acknowledge mistakes without sounding stupid. The ability to tell employees that you realize you could have given them more information or that you could have done something better shows them that you, too, know you are fallible AND are also able to apologize for errors. Even if you did not make a mistake, per se, but merely an oversight, you can't be expected to think of all the impacts of every situation. You will miss some things, that is, if you are human.

Probably one of the best things you can do to avoid burnout, and the costly mistakes in judgment that often accompany it, is to recognize its symptoms:

- ▶ Exhaustion

- ▶ Quick irritation

- ▶ Feelings of unworthiness or cynicism

- ▶ Poor decision making

Studies have shown that people who have to make many small decisions in a limited period of time often end up making bad ones toward the end. Good decisions need fresh brains!

If you recognize some of the symptoms of burnout in you, try taking yourself through a mental Exchange. It will not only give you a mental break, it will help you analyze the situation in the careful way that has been found to be so useful for dealing with conflicts. One result of burnout is less tolerance with yourself and others. When you find yourself losing patience with your colleagues or being overly self-critical, this is a perfect opportunity to reflect on the situational use of The Exchange methodology. So, if you are feeling overwhelmed and impatient with others, set aside a short amount of time and try this.

STAGE ONE: GATHER THE INFORMATION

Know your own *hot buttons*. What are the words or phrases that push you to react instead of respond? By consciously identifying them, you can put yourself on alert so that when you hear them (and you will), you can decide what to do and not blurt out something you will later regret.

Think about your *biases*. Do you shudder when someone complains about the cafeteria food? Or do you find a certain type of personality especially challenging? Again, knowing what bothers you *before* it comes up gives you the time to identify what you might do, for example, reminding yourself that a complainer is communicating in a way that has worked in the past and that it is not necessarily about you.

STAGE TWO: ANALYZE THE SITUATION

Some people find it helpful to write down the *key issues* that are causing them grief so they can really look at what to do to improve the situation. Others aren't quite so organized with their self-assessment.

Whether you write down the issues or just think about the issues you want to sort through, be sure to include thoughts about an *icebreaker* and the *impact* of what is going on with you. These two pieces will really help you put the issues you are having in the context of your values and your goals.

STAGE THREE: THINK THROUGH THE SITUATION

Start with reminding yourself about why you took your work position (the icebreaker) and why you love it. If you don't love it, maybe it's time to look at other possibilities, or at least consider changes you might make in your present situation. This exercise doesn't take more than a few seconds, but it provides an antidote to the negativity that may be consuming you.

Be honest about the impact the situation is having on you. Are you losing sleep? Are you finding yourself avoiding people? Is the situation taking up more mental space than it deserves?

Disaggregate the issues into smaller parts. This means breaking them down into smaller, more manageable ideas. Is the real issue not enough time, not enough information, not enough resources, or not enough people? Or is it all of the above?

How much of the situation is under your control? In other words, maybe part of the situation involves policies that are set by the hospital board or someone else. If you can't change policies, perhaps it's not helpful to spend too much time ruminating about them. If the policies should be changed, you will need allies. Who would they be?

If you don't have the ability, power, or energy to change the system, you *do* have control over your area and the people you supervise. A long-term employee of a large hospital acknowledged that the hospital was a very difficult place to work; there were problems at the top adversely affecting the tone of the organization and over which he had no control. Then he smiled and shared:

But I do have control over what happens in my department. And I am going to be the best damn manager these employees have ever had.

STAGE FOUR: EXPLORE YOUR OPTIONS

Don't try to do everything yourself. If you deny your team a chance to help resolve a situation, you are denying them a chance to grow and, more importantly, a chance to "own" the problem. Your team needs to recognize their stake in the joint effort, just as you do. As we have said before, participating in the process gives you a stake in the outcome. You need a team that recognizes their stake in the outcome. And they need to feel you trust them to do what is needed.

Finally, take a look at the balance in your life:

▶ Do you have time for your family and for a personal life?

▶ Do you have friends who are not medical providers?

▶ When was the last time you went to a regional or national conference and had the chance to socialize with peers?

▶ What would you do if you were not working and you could do anything you wanted to do?

Be as patient with yourself as you are with your team and with everyone else. If all of the above sounds a bit out of reach, just try a step or two and see how it feels. There are individuals who feel worthy only if they are busy. If this is you, it might be helpful to think how you are affecting the others in your life.

Radha and her son, Anan, had learned the importance of taking time for each other. She remembered an occasion, a year ago, when she discovered that he had been experimenting with drugs. In the course of dealing with the situation, she had been struck to learn that he thought he wasn't important to her life. From his perspective, her job was all that really mattered and she never had time for fun. She had taken his comments seriously and realized that she *had* become overinvolved at work and that she needed to step back from being the only go-to person in the Integrated Conflict Management System (ICMS).

Radha took her own advice and formed a team of facilitators, the chief one being Drew Johnson. It was Drew who had reminded her that the goal of The Exchange was to work with people, not just get things done. Her goal at the end of this day was *being* someone her son could talk to. You, of course, will have your own goals, and we encourage you to follow them.

CHAPTER 15

The Exchange: Will It Work at Home?

As she was leaving the gym, Radha Samson called her favorite pizzeria and ordered a large pizza with the "works." It was ready by the time she arrived to pick it up. Then she headed for home and for the conversation with her son, Anan. Use of the car was becoming a big issue.

Earlier that day Radha had received several excited text messages from Anan:

Mom, I need the car tomorrow. Have to go to Disneyland.

And then a minute later:

Mom, call back. Important.

"Yes," she had thought, "everything is important . . . but I can't deal with this right now." So she had texted back:

Let's talk tonight.

He answered her:

Okay, if I have to wait, but DON'T FORGET!

Her son could be as determined as she was! She wasn't really sure how to handle this latest challenge—the prospect of Anan driving 50 miles to the amusement park with a bunch, or even two, of his crazy friends. They were nice enough boys but not any more responsible than Anan, and she certainly didn't want them driving her car. She reluctantly realized that in only a year, Anan would be out of the house with no need to even ask for her permission. She decided to try a different approach this time.

As she drove up, the front door burst open and Radha watched her son and their dog, a German shepherd mix, race each other for the pizza box.

It didn't take long for Anan to raise the topic of the evening. He said:

So what about it, Mom? Peter's waiting for my call.

Instead of the instant rejection that she wanted to make—"you're too young, you're too inexperienced," etc.—Radha sat back and said:

I can see this is really a big deal for you. Tell me more. What are you thinking?

Anan began:

Well, Friday's an in-service day for the teachers, so we get it off and we figured the lines won't be as long as usual at Disneyland. So we're going. If I can have the car, that is.

Radha took a deep breath and, for a moment, forgot her resolution not to react, and then spoke:

Anan, you are just 17. You've only had your license a little over a year. Traffic can be very heavy on the way.

Anan responded:

Oh, Mom. You never trust me. You treat me as if I were still in junior high. What are you going to do when I'm 18 and a so-called adult?

Once again Radha took the bait and replied:

Look, Anan, I do have some worries. Besides the traffic and your lack of experience, I think your buddies can be very distracting. You have to be doubly focused when there is heavy traffic. And how would I get to work? And then, of course, what about the price of gas? Why don't you guys take the train?

Radha saw her son's face and remembered her determination to try The Exchange principles in her own conflict. She took a deep breath again and spoke:

Wait, Anan. I do know you are growing up and I know you are a good driver. It seems like you want me to trust you and recognize that you are almost an adult. You believe this is a perfect opportunity for you and your friends to enjoy your favorite place on earth! Do I get it?

Anan was a bit shocked. He knew she had a great reputation at work, but at home he felt that all she did was TELL him what to do. He grinned and said:

Yeah, actually you got it, Mom.

Anan's response was encouraging. Radha wondered why she couldn't always acknowledge him the way she did everyone else in her professional life. She always felt so much responsibility and love for him. How could she forget to do this? He had tested her in ways that his sister never had. She thought, "Let's see if it can still work," and told Anan:

I just can't help worrying. You're my son. So, let me give you a challenge. You know what my concerns are. Make me a proposal that meets my interests and you can take the car.

She thought this might be a good way to do it with Anan. He was so strong in his personality and so determined. She wanted to give him space, and, in a sense, have him do Stage Four (Problem Solving) on his own, so he would have to think through her perspective without her having to say any more about it. She suggested that they reconvene their discussion in an hour. Anan took his last piece of pizza into his room and Radha heard him talking to Peter about their discussion.

Twenty minutes later, Anan came back into the kitchen where Radha was reading the newspaper and announced that he was ready to resume the discussion. He began:

First, Mom. Safety. You're worried about me and traffic. So we'll leave after the morning rush hour. I looked online and it slows down after 8:30, so we'll leave at 9:00. That will give me time to drop you off at work, by the way. And then, just so you don't think I drove too fast, I'll call when we get there so you'll know I didn't go over the speed limit.

Radha was impressed. He actually had focused on her interest in safety, which was underlying the complaint about it being dangerous for him to drive. Maybe he would be a good interest-based negotiator someday after all! But, she wasn't done yet:

Thanks, Anan, I do appreciate your thoughts on this. One thing important to me is that you arrive home safely after a full day in the sun.

Anan announced:

We thought about that, and I knew you'd be concerned about the safety issue again, with all the cars on the road. We'll stay till after the evening rush—say about 7:30 or 8:00 p.m.—and then we'll call as we're leaving and you'll know when we get back. It'll be before 10 p.m., I promise.

Noticing his mother's raised eyebrows when he mentioned time, Anan added:

If you're worried about me falling asleep on the way home, we'll stop at McDonald's, the one about halfway from here. You know the one near the rest stop? If you don't believe me, we'll call you from there too.

And there are two more things—my distracting friends and gas money. Peter and Carlos will pay for the gas, ahead of time, to you. I can get it tonight. It seems like that would be fair, which I know is important to you. I am not sure how to deal with the distracting part. I won't let them drive and we can put the music only halfway up on the radio? They could take turns navigating? That would ensure that two of the three of us are focusing on the road. I don't quite know what to do about getting you home from work.

Entering into the spirit of problem solving, Radha replied:

That doesn't have to cause a problem. Drew Johnson lives in this direction and I'm sure he would give me a ride. In fact, I'll call him and check. I really appreciate how much you are trying to meet my interests. I think you understand that meeting my interests helps you get to Disneyland (a very important, lesson, Anan!). Let me think about your suggestions for a moment.

One thing she realized was that as a mother, especially as the mother of a son like Anan, she needed to think of all the possible problems that could come up because he had a good way of finding them. She had a responsibility that was much more personal than a manager to an employee. She didn't want to diminish the hard work Anan had done by seeming negative, but she wanted him to live up to what he had promised.

After thinking about Anan's suggestions, Radha spoke:

I think this is a great plan, but, one last thing. What if this doesn't work? What happens if there's a problem? If you're late, for example?

Anan looked troubled for a minute and then his eyes lit up:

Mom, if it doesn't work, you'll get your wish. I won't ask to drive for a month.

ADJUSTING THE EXCHANGE TO WORK AT HOME

Will The Exchange and its techniques work at home? With friends? With a little tweaking it can work in most conflicts. You will probably need to use a "stealth" tweak. Don't tell your son, your spouse, or your friend that you are going to try a conflict-resolution process "on" them. People don't want to be practiced on or be part of a system in which the other person is the expert. Especially if the conflict is heating up and you can tell that the other person is upset. Just do it!

Stage Two: Agenda Planning

Now that you have read a real-life example, let's put it in context and see how The Exchange was tweaked to work at home. Similar to addressing a disruptive employee (see Chapter 8) or a one-on-one situation, start with a Stage Two agenda-planning session alone. Think about what you want, need, and are hoping to gain from the conversation. Strategize about what might make the situation feel less like a confrontation and more like a discussion.

Radha brought home pizza as part of her strategy to make the discussion with her son, Anan, easier. She also took care to schedule the discussion for a time when both of them could focus. She did not react to his insistent text messages; rather, she responded in a way that made a more productive conversation possible. She could only imagine how a phone conversation while she was at work would have gone, with the pressures she felt there. The words "*I said no, Anan*," probably would have been uttered several times.

Radha also spent time thinking about how to frame her concerns in ways that Anan could accept. Even when she "lost it" a bit and went back to her old ways of interacting with him (old habits are hard to break), the fact that she had *planned* her responses and was conscious of her intentions made it possible for her to back off, apologize, and refocus.

STAGE ONE AND STAGE THREE: THE PRIVATE AND JOINT MEETINGS

So when you are both ready and comfortable, begin the discussion. Set up the situation so that there are not likely to be distractions and then go for it. But again, be strategic: don't start with your position or point of view. Ask for theirs.

Remember the Aikido concept described back in Chapter 9. The same principle is at work here, and it is even more important because emotional reactions are more likely to occur. Being an Aikidoist at home means *not reacting immediately* by telling someone he or she is wrong or by defending yourself. Instead, demonstrate that you got the other person's message by *repeating* or *paraphrasing* the major concern(s) you heard and/or *acknowledging* the person's challenges in the situation. Keep trying until you get some signal from the other person that he or she knows you have understood. There's often an almost magic moment of eye contact when it's clear that you got through to the other person.

Sometimes it may be an involuntary head nod and a relaxing of tense shoulders that demonstrates *she got it*. The power of this cannot be underestimated. It can transform the conversation.

This is a variant of a formal Exchange; you are combining Stage One and Stage Three. You've gathered important data that you might not have otherwise known or that you might have misinterpreted. If it's possible to insert a genuine compliment (Radha's acknowledgment about her son's driving, for example), it's like greasing a squeaky wheel.

But be careful that you don't sound condescending or phony. That would add another hurdle—the loss of trust. Trust can't be willed or decided on. Anan realized that if he didn't keep his part of the deal, it would take a long time for his mother to trust him with the car again.

After demonstrating that you understand and acknowledging the other's perspective, now it is time to lay your interests or concerns on the table in a nonconfrontational way. It is truly amazing how a non-judgmental statement of one's interests helps people hear what you need without causing them to take offense or become defensive.

When Radha said, *"One thing important to me is that you arrive home safely after a full day in the sun,"* she was stating her interests in a non-judgmental way. She had learned to do that with Anan the year before when he had a habit of dropping his shoes and his backpack on the living room floor when he got home from school. Her reaction to this had often been, *"Anan, how many times have I told you to . . ."* or *"You left a mess again."* These accusations were often met with defensiveness or excuses. She had decided she needed a new approach, so one day she simply said, *"I notice your sneakers are in the living room,"* and another day she declared with a light touch, *"You know your bedroom is your space, and for me, a neat living room really matters!"* Both times she was shocked at how he responded, *"Sorry, ma!"* while he removed the items. He gave no defense and no excuse. Magic! She knew she was on to something with stating her interests instead of complaining. Of course, it doesn't work for everything but she was increasingly turning to that approach, both at work and at home. Somehow, it was easier at work!

If you are not sure that the message you sent is what is was received, try saying something like:

It's really important to me that you understand that I'm not trying to . . . (whatever the person might predict your response would be).

You need to be sure that your real hopes and concerns have been heard. Otherwise, any resolution will not meet your needs and there is a great likelihood that the conflict will continue, even if it goes "underground."

STAGE FOUR: PROBLEM SOLVING

Then, and this is key to Stage Four, invite the other person to be part of the problem solving. It was Anan's participation in the final decision that almost guaranteed that the deal he made with his mother would work. One of the underlying principles of this process is that when people participate in the process, they have a stake in the outcome.

Will it be risky? Sure. Radha was still worried about her son's lack of driving experience, but she also knew that the potential gain of a stronger relationship would pay dividends in terms of trust when other difficult decisions came up as he made his way to manhood. If she didn't give him this chance, he would be more likely to find a less acceptable way to get his needs met. In her opinion, both Carlos and Peter were even less experienced drivers than Anan. She wanted to make sure that the boys were as safe as she could make them so it really was better if Anan drove. She also wanted to make sure that she was consulted in the future when her son faced challenges. She wanted him to know that she would take his concerns into account and that they were a team.

Disagreements, misunderstandings, and conflicts happen in the best of homes and friendships. Use techniques from The Exchange to sharpen your skills at communicating and demonstrating understanding. You may be surprised at the creative resolutions and the stronger relationships that result.

CHAPTER 16

Epilogue at St. Sonia's Hospital

Radha Samson and Drew Johnson sat facing each other at the end of the long conference table in St. Sonia's Business Office. They had paper and open computers in front of them, as well as cups of hot hospital coffee. They were preparing for their joint presentation to the hospital board on the effects of three years of The Exchange process at St Sonia's Hospital.

Radha began by suggesting:

Let's start with the stories. If our goal is to demonstrate that we now operate—pun intended—in a different culture than we did three years ago, we need to set the scene. We can get to the factual evidence and the bottom line later; but I want them to really understand how and why it is so powerful.

Drew responded:

I agree. We can't talk about the private conversations because of confidentiality, but we can certainly talk about the resulting changes in protocols, procedures, and policies that have resulted.

Radha added:

Yes, and the people. The people: those who have been affected by participating and the facilitators who have been part of the process and part of the joint problem solving.

Drew continued:

Okay, let's start with a few of the most influential cases. We've talked to each other about some of those and I think we need to include Kim Brown's case about the nurses' station as well as the couple that the Patient Relations Department facilitated.

Radha was organizing in her head as she remembered what a long way they had come from the first training session, three years ago, and the skepticism she and the other team members had faced from the hospital board and from the department heads. Radha suggested:

So let's pick eight or ten more dramatic ones. By that I mean the ones that affected the most people, and focus on the results of each.

After a few minutes of brainstorming, they decided to pick:

▶ Two classic cases involving one manager and two employees

▶ Two cases illustrating how to work with groups

▶ Two cases involving patients as participants

▶ Two cases focusing on patient families

▶ Two cases involving disruptive individual employees

These were the cases they chose:

▶ ***Room Transfer.*** One of Radha's first cases between RN Kim Brown and hospital financial donor and patient, Marvin Yee (Chapter 11). The resolution of the conflict over responsiveness of staff and patient input had included a new protocol that assured patients that they had been heard and gave nurses and other staff members a chance to make reasoned decisions. It had also resulted in Kim taking The Exchange training and becoming one of the hospital's most competent facilitators. Because of his experience, Mr. Yee had made a special donation to The Exchange Program to cover Advanced Training for all members of the Patient Relations Department as well as the Ombuds team that worked in tandem with the Patient Relations Department.

- *Missed Appointment.* A case from the clinic between Physician's Assistant John Chu and Front Desk Scheduler Lilly Brown (Chapter 7) resulted in a change of protocols during particularly busy times. Appointments were rescheduled by the front desk staff only after consulting with the provider. Providers agreed to answer calls about scheduling as soon as possible and to give the scheduler two choices of new times, including the opportunity to be fit the patient into the current day's timeframe. Aside from written policy notes to patients about schedules, if a problem arose, the patient needing the appointment would be asked to wait in a small office near the desk and told about the new protocol.

- *The Nurses' Station* (Chapters 3, 4, 5, 6). This was a recent case but it illustrated how far-reaching an agreement could be. The "shrine" that RN Yvette Jones had alluded to was gone. A bulletin board behind the desk had been installed and became a central communication vehicle for all of the nurses, with a committee formed to monitor and update items as needed. RN Simon Peters had passed his seminar on IV Competency and no longer hesitated to administer them. There had been no complaints from either patients or supervising nurses. Yvette had also attended a seminar on the importance of bedside manner and it had affected not only her dealing with patients but extended to colleagues who appreciated the new warmth she exuded. The nursing department had caught the spirit of congenial cooperation and now held a bimonthly social event to give their members more opportunities to develop personal connections with the result of greater trust and willingness to consult among department nurses.

- *Intradepartment Scheduling* (Chapter 13). What started as a private first meeting with technicians in the lab became a departmental facilitation about coverage and about dealing with unrealistic deadlines from other departments. The resulting memos to the rest of the hospital, as well as the empowerment of the front desk staff to be responsible for their own break coverage, became models for other departments in terms of group decision making. Better morale in the lab was evident to anyone who stopped by. It seemed that as technicians felt respected by colleagues in other departments, they responded more positively to urgent requests in emergency situations and more competently in explaining why delays occurred or when they were unable to comply with requests.

▶ ***Shared Equipment*** (Chapter 13). Radha was particularly pleased at how the joint discussion between ICU and Hospice staff had taken place. The unique equipment sharing agreement, which also provided for joint oversight of most commonly used machines, became a model for other departments. A whole-hospital committee has been set up to handle joint use in a number of different situations. The committee is slated to convene next month and will include representatives from nursing, technicians, physicians, nonmedical, and administrative staff. The family that was distraught over the conflict between the two departments, and the potential impact on their loved one, was relieved to learn that new protocols had been put in place to manage the equipment and to ease tension between the departments, which would alleviate any problems for future families.

▶ ***Unnecessary Surgery*** (Chapter 11). This case represented a landmark for St. Sonia's Hospital. It was the first case in which an alleged medical error had been addressed in an Exchange process by the primary parties prior to the filing of a lawsuit. Risk Management had been supportive of "the experiment" but doubtful that it would succeed in an agreement. When it did, attorneys for the hospital began to recommend it in other situations. The creative solution of a task force for women who had concerns about diagnoses or treatment, made up of both providers and former patients, was getting off to a good start. In fact, Dr. Ivan Petraeus had been joined in his "training" project by other physicians, including a surgeon who had been sued successfully five years ago. The ombuds who facilitated the process were delighted with the results and had encouraged other ombuds to sign up for future Exchange training.

▶ *Prescribing Antibiotics* (Chapter 12). The Exchange process between a patient's father (William Carson) and the nurse practitioner (Tanya Stewart) who had opted not to prescribe antibiotics had been facilitated by a member of the Patient Relations Department (Betsy Rose). It had focused on each party describing his or her expectations to each other and concluded with a handshake. However, the most important result had been a recommitment to her profession by the young nurse practitioner who had been devastated by the whole situation and contemplated ending her healthcare career.

▶ *End-of-Life Decisions* (Chapter 12). This Exchange, facilitated by the Patient Relations Department's Exchange team, was a unique case as no providers were included, but the hospital had been able to help two family members (a patient's wife and mother) deal with a very emotional issue—whether or not to end life support for a relative. They had not been able to talk to each other prior to The Exchange, yet a decision was required. Both women wanted to be able to justify their point of view to the other. In the end, the young man had been removed from the machines and passed away 18 hours later with both women at his side.

▶ *Computer Whiz* (Chapter 8). Radha had used The Exchange techniques to work with a brilliant but difficult technician who had made unpleasant ripples throughout the hospital.

Adjusting The Exchange process by combining Stage One with Stages Three and Four, Radha met one-on-one with the young computer specialist. Because he was treated respectfully but honestly, he was able to think about the consequences of his style and decided that he would rather stay at St. Sonia's—where he had a chance to advance—than take a chance on some other institution where his abrasiveness would lead to immediate dismissal. He couldn't agree to change his personality, but he did agree to boundaries and to use Radha as a sounding board for new encounters. He also agreed to work with his supervisor to find times for using his "magic" with computers when the user was out of the office, relying on e-mails for communication. After checking with his supervisor, Radha was able to report that the agreement appeared to be working.

► *Food Service* (Chapter 10). The other one-on-one variation on The Exchange had been facilitated by Drew and involved an employee dealing with an abusive boss. The results of this process ended with the employee (Esther Cabrera) making a carefully thought-out decision not to challenge her boss but to keep a low profile until she could find another situation, which she did two months later. She left the process feeling empowered to make a choice, not as a victim. Her decision involved a consideration of how her children and husband were being affected by the status quo. Drew noted that his session with Esther's boss, in which he adapted The Exchange process to work with a disruptive employee (Emily Smith), had been successful. She was able to take responsibility for her mistakes and later received additional management training so she could improve her skills.

As they finished their discussion about cases, Drew leaned over to his colleague Radha and in a somewhat teasing tone suggested that she mention how The Exchange techniques had affected her relationship with her 17-year-old son. Radha countered:

Maybe, but I don't want to sound like a zealot. Maybe it would be better if I just quote some of our other fellow facilitators who have recounted the importance of using these techniques outside the office.

Drew replied:

Yes, and then you could mention that our facilitator group has grown from the first six to twenty-five. I think every aspect of the hospital has been involved in at least one training.

Radha added:

Good idea, and we can then talk about the advanced group that we call on for complex, interdepartmental cases—the folks in Patient Relations or in the Ombuds program, for example.

Drew injected:

Don't forget the communication skills trainings for front-line staff. I think it's made a real difference in how staff, in general, treat each other and that seems to have also influenced how they deal with patients. Everything goes back to good health care on some level. And what about the famous bottom line*? What can we say about the business end of The Exchange?*

Radha responded:

Well, that is a relatively easy topic. We can certainly point to the fact that employee turnover has been reduced. While it is hard to measure a negative, the fact that we don't have to spend money on orienting and training so many new hires—not to say we don't have any new hires; we are expanding and growing, and people need to leave for good reasons. But for now we don't seem to face the morale problems of dysfunctional departments. Even more interesting is that we can show records that fewer days off for stress are being requested. I think you keep those stats? So maybe our own staff is healthier!

When Drew nodded that he could provide that information, Radha continued:

I do think though that we need to be careful not to sound too "Pollyanna-ish." The Exchange is not magic or the answer to every issue that comes up, but it sure has been more practical than I would have believed. We clearly still have conflicts. We're not Pleasantville, *thank goodness. That might be really boring.*

Drew concurred and continued:

Oh yeah, I had to deal with a justified firing last week and found myself wishing for that magic wand. I think if the guy had been willing to engage in an Exchange, and by the way, we offered him one six months ago, he might at least have left on better terms. As it was, he was not a happy camper. And, of course, patients and their families still occasionally complain. But not nearly as much as before. It's really a different world.

Radha stopped him and remarked:

You know I just realized that in some ways we have a whole new culture here at St. Sonia's. We've joked about being a tiny island nation with our own customs and history, our own system of government even, and of course, our own economy. From my position, it looks as if this little nation is doing better than even I expected three years ago! I'm looking forward to the Board meeting.

Appendixes

Communication Skills for the Exchange

KEY TOOL FOR STAGE ONE: EFFECTIVE LISTENING

The Exchange begins with effective listening. Most of us assume that listening is an instinct; it is something that we know how to do without trying. It's also pretty clear that almost from birth we also want other people to listen to us. Babies cry to alert a parent that something is needed—a dry diaper or a mouthful of milk. And yet, it is also clear that some listening is not very effective. If you have or are familiar with children, you have probably witnessed a scene involving a toddler tugging on a parent's leg or arm or anything "tuggable" and demanding attention. "Listen to me" is the unspoken plea.

If listening is not an instinct, at least it is something we learn very early. Remember your parent demanding, "Listen to me, young lady"? And yet, in our experience, most conflicts begin because someone feels that he or she has been ignored, misinterpreted, or treated disrespectfully by someone else who didn't really *listen* to him or her. We've also observed that in many situations, the "other" party actually was listening but not *effectively listening*.

Multitasking may be an important skill in this complex multi-demanding world of health care but to be effective in managing conflict, one must at least give the appearance of providing full, undivided attention. In the beginning, you may just have to act like you are paying attention. Be assured, emotions often follow behaviors and soon you will be fully present for the other person. And you will have developed a skill that will earn you great rewards. A skill that can be practiced and improved so that you actually *are* paying attention!

Most human beings want to understand other people and be understood by other people. We want the messages we send to be received in the spirit in which they were intended. We also want to know that the real message, the meta-message of the feelings behind the words, was received. Overall, we want to know that someone has really listened to us. One doctor told us that he didn't understand his staff. When the staff complained about things, he would quickly analyze the problem and give them his best solution, sometimes what they said they wanted. He was puzzled that they often left his office unhappy until one staff member said that she wasn't looking for his quick and abrupt answer, she wanted him to *actually* hear her out and acknowledge her experience, not just fix it for her. The way in which he listened felt dismissive, and his answers were hasty, so she was never sure he understood the true issues.

So what is *effective listening*? We define it as when the speaker believes that he or she has been heard because the listener demonstrates certain behaviors. It's not as easy as it sounds. In fact, to be really effective, there are logical steps to effective listening that can be learned. In normal conversation, one does not have to go through each step; our friends usually give us some slack. But in a conflict they can make the difference between resolution and escalation. Below are four steps to effective listening when it really matters.

STOP WHATEVER YOU ARE DOING AND TURN TOWARD THE PERSON

Body language is indeed a language that involves sending and receiving unspoken messages. While you can hear someone who is talking to you without looking at the speaker, if you are in the same physical space and you claim to be listening to someone but there is no change in your posture, the message to the speaker is some variant of the following:

▶ "She really doesn't want to hear what I have to say."

▶ "What I have to say is not as important as what he is doing."

If you are caught unaware by the other person, or if you have an appointment in a few minutes, or you are involved in something you can't stop, don't even start a substantive conversation. But do make sure that the other person understands why and set a time, as soon as possible, when you will be able to listen effectively, and not have to keep glancing at your watch or at the papers on your desk.

We suggest that your body language should reflect interest. One way to do this is to lean slightly forward. If you are standing, sit down and invite the other person to do likewise. Then lean forward and make "friendly" eye contact. By that we mean connect with the person, but don't stare!

Eye contact is an interesting phenomenon. For most Americans, direct eye contact is often considered a sign that the truth is being told. People who don't make direct eye contact risk being considered "shifty" or trying to hide something. For many other cultures, however, too much eye contact may be taken as disrespect or aggression, especially if the eye contact is maintained for more than a second or two. In listening, the message of initial eye contact is, "You are important and I want to know what you have to tell me." After the first contact, you will probably sense what is appropriate; just don't turn away and back to your desk!

FOCUS ON THE OTHER PERSON'S BODY LANGUAGE, AS WELL AS ON THE PERSON'S WORDS.

Notice if the person seems uncomfortable, edgy, or nervous. Then do something to make the climate more comfortable. For example, shake or extend a hand palm up (some cultures frown on touching between men and women) in a gesture of welcome, stand up in greeting, or just smile warmly as you make eye contact. If you are sitting behind a desk, consider coming out from behind what may seem like a barrier and sit so that there is nothing between you and the speaker. Too often, desks are symbols of power and the person who is behind the desk is the powerful one. Regardless of your professional position, in successful conflict resolution, all parties have equal opportunities to talk and to participate in making decisions.

If your goal is to manage a conflict situation successfully (that is, without escalation), adjust your body language to project the message that this is a safe space in which important conversations can take place. When you adopt a posture that is comfortable (or actually even that is uncomfortable), an interesting thing happens. When the other person sees this position or a facial gesture such as a smile, neurons fire in his or her brain, mirroring the same gesture that you are sending to him or her. Aptly named *mirror neurons*, this firing of neurons in the brain informs the person of how to react appropriately in a given situation.

The mirror neurons are in the section of the brain directing a particular behavior. When the neurons perceive an action by someone else, they light up as if they were performing the action. Think about yawns. One person yawns and soon it looks as if everyone else is about to start a nap.

There is also an automatic, unconscious tendency to mimic posture. Test this by crossing your legs sometime and see who else soon follows the pattern. How you sit and what you look like affect both of you. There are some studies of communication in conflict that indicate 55 percent of what a person takes away from a conflict is the body language (not the words, which only account for 7 percent of what people remember). This is especially true when the body language and tone do not match the words. If there is inconsistency between body language and what the person is saying, people tend to believe the body language. Nonverbal actions matter!

Invite the Person to Talk.

An easy way to do this is directly. After the nonsubstantive but important civilities of making the person feel comfortable, it's time to find out why he or she is there. So ask. If the person is obviously agitated you could ask, "What's wrong?" Sometimes, there aren't a lot of clues except the physical presence of the other person. So then you might try a little lighter invitation like, "What's up?" The point is that people are more likely to start talking if they are invited to do so.

Hear the Story without Substantive Comment

It may seem obvious that listeners don't talk. Unfortunately, many times people don't consider their comments to be interruptive talk. They immediately ask a penetrating question or offer a bit of advice or, worse still, justify their own or someone else's actions! All those things might be needed and there is a place for some of them later. But first, the speaker needs space that is uniquely his or hers. Whatever your good intentions, *any* interruption is likely to distort the original communication and distract the speaker or cause him or her to lose the thread of his or her concern.

This doesn't mean you maintain a stony silence. There are lots of encouraging sounds you can make that help the flow. "Uh-huh" or "hmm" are just a couple. And the look on your face should mirror the emotional content of what is being said (remember that the mirror neurons work both ways). But mostly, just sit comfortably and listen! You'll have an opportunity to respond in a minute. The more you try to take your turn before the speaker is finished, the harder it will be to get him or her to stop talking or he or she will just shut down and you'll miss the real point of the conversation.

DISTANCE LISTENING

What do you do if you are on the phone instead of in the same room? While it seems obvious that the most effective listening takes place face-to-face, when you can see each other and take note of body language, it is possible to be effective if you are not in the same physical space. In such situations of "distance-conversations" your most helpful tool will be tone. *Tone* refers to pitch, volume, pacing—all those sensory additions to the words that are too often undervalued. By some estimates, what people in conflict remember from a conversation is 38 percent tone. Over a phone, that percentage is even more important. And those encouraging little nonword sounds referred to above are even more important. The basic rules still apply:

- ▸ Try to make the person comfortable.

- ▸ Assure the person that you want to hear what he or she has to say.

- ▸ Invite the person to talk.

Tone in an E-mail or a Text Message

What kind of tone can you project in an e-mail or a text message? This is indeed an issue. Tone is often represented by capital letters, boldface letters, or letters in a special font. Most of us have discovered the beauty of electronic media in terms of speed and efficiency of exchanging information. Most of us have also experienced the embarrassments that are part of this type of communication such as pushing the "reply to all" button, when we really only wanted to respond to one person or rushing off a reply in capital letters to what seemed like an insult, before reflecting on the reply.

If you are involved in such a conflict or asked to get involved between two people for whom e-mail has resulted in a conflict, we suggest that you make every effort to get everyone in the same room or if necessary on the same conference call or video conference. *A cautionary note:* Don't try text messaging as a method for short-circuiting the opportunity to listen in on a conflict! Use text messaging only to schedule a meeting or to change a date.

AFTER LISTENING, RESPOND RESPECTFULLY

After listening, a real conversation requires a response. A key skill for facilitators of The Exchange is making a respectful response that leads to either more information or the beginning of a solution. But first, the response must make clear to the speaker that the message sent was the one received. There are three steps.

Demonstrate Understanding

Unless the speaker believes he or she has actually been heard in the way he or she wants to be heard, the speaker will continue to repeat his or her complaints and with each repetition underscore his or her own version of the issues. Once the speaker feels understood, he or she can move beyond the history to think about other aspects of the situation. So how do you do this? The answer is quite simple, but not so easy. The skill is *paraphrasing*. This means to repeat the KEY point of the speaker's story in different words than he or she used.

It is important not to retell the whole complaint. If you do, you are likely to distract the speaker, who will want to correct every detail or add to specifics. The key point is easily lost in details. When you do identify the key concerns and want to show that indeed you do understand, use different words; this is proof that you are not just mimicking the speaker or even worse, that you are too dense to really get the speaker's words. So use your own words and then check for accuracy. You can say something like *"Did I get it?"* or *"Is that what you wanted me to hear?"*

If there is a nod or a word of agreement, you are ready to move to the next step. If you haven't quite gotten it, don't worry; the speaker will be happy to clarify. After all, there are few more flattering occasions than someone trying sincerely to understand you!

ACKNOWLEDGE THE IMPACT

Unless there is an emotional component, most conflicts do not escalate; they are just not that important. But when someone feels treated badly or unfairly, the conflict almost always grows. Acknowledging the emotional effect need not be belabored, but doing so makes a tremendous difference. Here are some sentences that almost always work:

▶ *It sounds like that was hard for you to hear.*

▶ *That must have been really tough.*

▶ *How frustrating for you.*

▶ *It seems like I really disappointed you.*

Acknowledging the person's feelings makes a huge difference if the words are delivered sincerely. You may notice a change in body language such as relaxed shoulders or increased eye contact. Then you can move smoothly on to the next step.

IDENTIFY THE INTERESTS

Here is the real magic of respectful responding. It demonstrates a deeper listening than often happens. The goal of this step is to guess at what the speaker really wanted out of the encounter. *Interests* are the unstated hopes, fears, and concerns that underlie the conflict. They are the motivations or expectations that make a person become involved in a conflict. By bringing the interests to the surface, the speaker has the opportunity to see how the conflict might have been different and thereby sets up the first step to resolution—something that will meet those hopes and needs. You don't have to be exactly on target; just trying is helpful in getting the speaker to examine his or her role in the conflict. Begin your guess with something like:

▶   *You were hoping that she would . . . ?*

▶   *You would have liked her to . . . ?*

▶   *What you wanted from me was better communication about . . . ?*

▶   *Did you want me to give you a chance for input before I . . . ?*

As discussed in Chapter 3, common workplace interests will often be found by listening more deeply to the complaints of the person. If the manager can listen for the underlying workplace needs and interests of the employee, he or she can go a long way toward encouraging solutions that create a better work environment for everyone. Not surprisingly, the common workplace interests that are encountered in healthcare settings include:

▶   Respectful treatment

▶   Acceptance of different work styles

▶   Fairness

▶   Acknowledgment for contributions

▶   Safe work environment

▶   Patient safety

▸ Trust

▸ Teamwork

▸ Fair workload

REACTION TO THE "RESPOND RESPECTFULLY" TECHNIQUE OF THE EXCHANGE

Someone who was familiar with these techniques once revealed something deeply personal about her perception of the use of these techniques. She said that her father had been in Alcoholics Anonymous for her entire childhood and so she had learned a great deal about its Twelve Step methodology. She had decided that they were powerful ideas for anyone to learn and grow from, not just alcoholics. She felt if everyone did the Twelve Steps the world could change. She said that when she learned and began to utilize the "Respond Respectfully" techniques of The Exchange it was the second time in her life that she had the feeling that if people used these ideas the world could change. We are not sure if the world can be changed with these principles, but we are fairly certain that your world of managing conflict will be improved.

THEN, GO DEEPER WITH QUESTIONS

Questions can be traps, especially if they are really statements in disguise or covering up advice. Questions can make people feel as if they have been subjected to cross-examinations or are being called names. However, some questions can be door openers. They can allow a person the freedom to say more about a personal subject or just feel invited to the conversation. These are the questions that facilitate communication. In general they come in two categories: open and closed questions.

OPEN QUESTIONS

Open questions are questions that can't be answered in one or two words. They are the questions that a facilitator in The Exchange would ask in a search for a solution that met everyone's needs.

1. In Stage One, they would be questions or requests designed to elicit more information from each party. Here are examples:
   - *Please tell me the situation from your perspective.*
   - *Could you say a little more about that?*
   - *Help me understand how you reached that conclusion*
   - *I didn't quite get what you meant, could you explain?*

2. In Stage Two, they would be unspoken questions that you ask yourself as you construct an agenda. Here are examples:
   - *What did I learn about each one's underlying interests?*
   - *How is this situation affecting each of them?*
   - *What could I say to break the ice?*

3. In Stage Three, open questions are a bit different. Here the goal is to get the participants to speak comfortably and openly with each other, yet on only one subject at a time. Open questions also help to break down barriers of hurt feelings because they provide an opportunity for each person to see the other in a different light—the light of how he or she saw him- or herself. Here are examples:
   - *How has this affected you?* Do not ask for the person's entire perspective about the situation.
   - *Would you please tell us your thoughts about . . .?* Name only one subject at a time.

4. In Stage Four, the questions would concern solutions. Here are examples:
   - *How could we resolve this?*
   - *What would you be willing to do?*
   - *What shall we say to the rest of the department?*

CLOSED QUESTIONS

Closed questions are questions that require a one- or two-word answer. They can be quite useful to verify facts, but they are not very helpful in gaining new information or in making speakers feel comfortable. In The Exchange, closed questions are generally most helpful in Stages Three and Four in narrowing options, checking for accuracy, and securing commitments. Here are examples:

▶ *So does this cover what we need?*

▶ *When can you be there?*

▶ *Is that what you wanted him to hear?*

"Why" Questions

While most conversations in The Exchange will include greater understanding of motivations and goals, a blunt "why" question hardly ever does the job. "Why" questions usually defeat their purpose by making the person you are asking feel defensive and reluctant to say more than absolutely necessary. The trick is to find out why without asking directly. Try these instead:

▶ *I'd like to understand. Please tell me how you got to that conclusion.*

▶ *It sounds as if this is very important to you. Could you say more?*

▶ *It would be really helpful to know what you were expecting.*

CONCLUSION

Good communication is more than words or questions. But carefully chosen words and good questions do help. The attitude conveyed with the questions is paramount. We suggest that a *curious* attitude works best, rather than a quasi-interrogation.

The combination of listening effectively, responding respectively, and asking nonthreatening questions work together in The Exchange and in life when situations become tense or stressful. One manager noted that The Exchange methodology not only helped her when conflicts arose in the clinic she managed, but also helped her communicate with her staff better on an ongoing basis.

Sentinel Event Alert

July 9, 2008, Issue 40

[*Editor's Note: Numbers in parentheses refer to the numbered reference list at the end of this article.*]

BEHAVIORS THAT UNDERMINE A CULTURE OF SAFETY

Intimidating and disruptive behaviors can foster medical errors (1, 2, 3), contribute to poor patient satisfaction and preventable adverse outcomes (1, 4, 5), increase the cost of care (4, 5), and cause qualified clinicians, administrators, and managers to seek new positions in more professional environments (1, 6). Safety and quality of patient care is dependent on teamwork, communication, and a collaborative work environment. To assure quality and to promote a culture of safety, healthcare organizations must address the problem of behaviors that threaten the performance of the healthcare team.

Intimidating and disruptive behaviors include overt actions such as verbal outbursts and physical threats, as well as passive activities such as refusing to perform assigned tasks or quietly exhibiting uncooperative attitudes during routine activities. Intimidating and disruptive behaviors are often manifested by healthcare professionals in positions of power. Such behaviors include reluctance or refusal to answer questions, return phone calls or pages, condescending language or voice intonation, and impatience with questions (2). Overt and passive behaviors undermine team effectiveness and can compromise the safety of patients (7, 8, 11). All intimidating and disruptive behaviors are unprofessional and should not be tolerated.

Intimidating and disruptive behaviors in healthcare organizations are not rare (1, 2, 7, 8, 9). A survey on intimidation conducted by the Institute for Safe Medication Practices found that 40 percent of clinicians have kept quiet or remained passive during patient care events rather than question a known intimidator (2, 10). While most formal research centers on intimidating and disruptive behaviors among physicians and nurses, there is evidence that these behaviors occur among other healthcare professionals, such as pharmacists, therapists, and support staff, as well as among administrators (1, 2). Several surveys have found that most care providers have experienced or witnessed intimidating or disruptive behaviors (1, 2, 8, 12, 13). These behaviors are not limited to one gender and occur during interactions within and across disciplines (1, 2, 7). Nor are such behaviors confined to the small number of individuals who habitually exhibit them (2). It is likely that these individuals are not involved in the large majority of episodes of intimidating or disruptive behaviors. It is important that organizations recognize that it is the behaviors that threaten patient safety, irrespective of who engages in them.

The majority of healthcare professionals enter their chosen discipline for altruistic reasons and have a strong interest in caring for and helping other human beings. The preponderance of these individuals carry out their duties in a manner consistent with this idealism and maintain high levels of professionalism. The presence of intimidating and disruptive behaviors in an organization, however, erodes professional behavior and creates an unhealthy or even hostile work environment—one that is readily recognized by patients and their families. Healthcare organizations that ignore these behaviors also expose themselves to litigation from both employees and patients. Studies link patient complaints about unprofessional, disruptive behaviors and malpractice risk (13, 14, 15). "Any behavior which impairs the healthcare team's ability to function well creates risk," says Gerald Hickson, M.D., associate dean for Clinical Affairs and director of the Center for Patient and Professional Advocacy at Vanderbilt University Medical Center. "If healthcare organizations encourage patients and families to speak up, their observations and complaints, if recorded and fed back to organizational leadership, can serve as part of a surveillance system to identify behaviors by members of the healthcare team that create unnecessary risk."

ROOT CAUSES AND CONTRIBUTING FACTORS

There is a history of tolerance and indifference to intimidating and disruptive behaviors in health care (10). Organizations that fail to address unprofessional behavior through formal systems are indirectly promoting it (9, 11). Intimidating and disruptive behavior stems from both individual and systemic factors (4). The inherent stresses of dealing with high-stakes, high-emotion situations can contribute to occasional intimidating or disruptive behavior, particularly in the presence of factors such as fatigue. Individual care providers who exhibit characteristics such as self-centeredness, immaturity, or defensiveness can be more prone to unprofessional behavior (8, 11). They can lack interpersonal, coping, or conflict management skills.

Systemic factors stem from the unique healthcare cultural environment, which is marked by pressures that include increased productivity demands, cost containment requirements, embedded hierarchies, and fear of or stress from litigation. These pressures can be further exacerbated by changes to or differences in the authority, autonomy, empowerment, and roles or values of professionals on the healthcare team (5, 7, 16), as well as by the continual flux of daily changes in shifts, rotations, and interdepartmental support staff. This dynamic creates challenges for inter-professional communication and for the development of trust among team members.

Disruptive behaviors often go unreported, and therefore unaddressed, for a number of reasons. Fear of retaliation and the stigma associated with "blowing the whistle" on a colleague, as well as a general reluctance to confront an intimidator all contribute to underreporting of intimidating and/or disruptive behavior (2, 9, 12, 16). Additionally, staff within institutions often perceive that powerful, revenue-generating physicians are "let off the hook" for inappropriate behavior due to the perceived consequences of confronting them (8, 10, 12, 17). The American College of Physician Executives (ACPE) conducted a physician behavior survey and found that 38.9 percent of the respondents agreed that "physicians in my organization who generate high amounts of revenue are treated more leniently when it comes to behavior problems than those who bring in less revenue"(17).

EXISTING JOINT COMMISSION REQUIREMENTS

Effective January 1, 2009, for all accreditation programs, The Joint Commission has a new Leadership standard, LD.03.01.01. During development, this standard was numbered LD.3.10. This standard addresses disruptive and inappropriate behaviors in two of its elements of performance:

- ▸ **EP 4:** The hospital/organization has a code of conduct that defines acceptable and disruptive and inappropriate behaviors.

- ▸ **EP 5**: Leaders create and implement a process for managing disruptive and inappropriate behaviors.

In addition, standards in the Medical Staff chapter have been organized to follow six core competencies (see the introduction) to be addressed in the credentialing process, including interpersonal skills and professionalism.

OTHER JOINT COMMISSION SUGGESTED ACTIONS

1. Educate all team members—both physicians and nonphysician staff—on appropriate professional behavior defined by the organization's code of conduct. The code and education should emphasize respect. Include training in basic business etiquette (particularly phone skills) and people skills (10, 18, 19).

2. Hold all team members accountable for modeling desirable behaviors, and enforce the code consistently and equitably

among all staff, regardless of seniority or clinical discipline, in a positive fashion through reinforcement as well as punishment (2, 4, 9, 10, 11).

3. Develop and implement policies and procedures/processes appropriate for the organization that address:
   - "Zero tolerance" for intimidating and/or disruptive behaviors, especially the most egregious instances of disruptive behavior such as assault and other criminal acts. Incorporate the zero tolerance policy into medical staff bylaws and employment agreements as well as administrative policies.
   - Medical staff policies regarding intimidating and/or disruptive behaviors of physicians within a healthcare organization should be complementary and supportive of the policies that are present in the organization for non-physician staff.
   - Reducing fear of intimidation or retribution and protecting those who report or cooperate in the investigation of intimidating, disruptive, and other unprofessional behavior (10, 18). Nonretaliation clauses should be included in all policy statements that address disruptive behaviors.
   - Responding to patients and/or their families who are involved in or witness intimidating and/or disruptive behaviors. The response should include hearing and empathizing with their concerns, thanking them for sharing those concerns, and apologizing (11).
   - How and when to begin disciplinary actions (such as suspension, termination, loss of clinical privileges, reports to professional licensure bodies).

4. Develop an organizational process for addressing intimidating and disruptive behaviors (LD.3.10 EP 5) that solicits and integrates substantial input from an inter-professional team including representation of medical and nursing staff, administrators, and other employees (4, 10, 18).

5. Provide skills-based training and coaching for all leaders and managers in relationship-building and collaborative

practice, including skills for giving feedback on unprofessional behavior, and conflict resolution (4, 7, 10, 11, 17, 20) . Cultural assessment tools can also be used to measure whether or not attitudes change over time.

6. Develop and implement a system for assessing staff perceptions of the seriousness and extent of instances of unprofessional behaviors and the risk of harm to patients (10, 17, 18).

7. Develop and implement a reporting/surveillance system (possibly anonymous) for detecting unprofessional behavior. Include ombuds services (20) and patient advocates (2, 11), both of which provide important feedback from patients and families who may experience intimidating or disruptive behavior from health professionals. Monitor system effectiveness through regular surveys, focus groups, peer and team member evaluations, or other methods (10). Have multiple and specific strategies to learn whether intimidating or disruptive behaviors exist or recur, such as through direct inquiries at routine intervals with staff, supervisors, and peers.

8. Support surveillance with tiered, nonconfrontational interventional strategies, starting with informal "cup of coffee" conversations directly addressing the problem and moving toward detailed action plans and progressive discipline, if patterns persist (4, 5, 10, 11). These interventions should initially be non-adversarial in nature, with the focus on building trust, placing accountability on and rehabilitating the offending individual, and protecting patient safety (4, 5). Make use of mediators and conflict coaches when professional dispute resolution skills are needed (4, 7, 14).

9. Conduct all interventions within the context of an organizational commitment to the health and well-being of all staff (11), with adequate resources to support individuals whose behavior is caused or influenced by physical or mental health pathologies.

10. Encourage inter-professional dialogues across a variety of forums as a proactive way of addressing ongoing conflicts, overcoming them, and moving forward through improved collaboration and communication (1, 2, 4, 10).

11. Document all attempts to address intimidating and disruptive behaviors (18).

REFERENCES

[Editor's Note: This reference list is reproduced as found in the original article. The numbers of items refer to the numbered callouts in parentheses in the text preceding.]

1. Rosenstein, A. H., and O'Daniel, M. "Disruptive behavior and clinical outcomes: Perceptions of nurses and physicians." American Journal of Nursing 2005,105, no.1: 54–64.
2. Institute for Safe Medication Practices: Survey on workplace intimidation. (2003). Available online: https://ismp.org/Survey/surveyresults/Survey0311.asp (accessed April 14, 2008).
3. Morrissey, J. "Encyclopedia of errors; Growing database of medication errors allows hospitals to compare their track records with facilities nationwide in a nonpunitive setting." Modern Healthcare (March 24, 2003)33(12): 40, 42.
4. Gerardi, D. "Effective strategies for addressing 'disruptive' behavior: Moving from avoidance to engagement." Medical Group Management Association Webcast, 2007; and Gerardi, D. "Creating cultures of engagement: effective strategies for addressing conflict and 'disruptive' behavior." Arizona Hospital Association Annual Patient Safety Forum, 2008.
5. Ransom, S. B., Neff, K.E., et al. "Enhancing physician performance," American College of Physician Executives, Tampa, FL, 2000. See Chapter 4, pp. 45–72.
6. Rosenstein, A., et al. "Disruptive physician behavior contributes to nursing shortage: Study links bad behavior by doctors to nurses leaving the profession." Physician Executive (November/December 2002), 28(6): 8–11. Available online: http://findarticles.com/p/articles/mi_m0843/is_6_28/ai_94590407 (accessed April 14, 2008)
7. Gerardi, D. "The emerging culture of health care: Improving end-of-life care through collaboration and conflict engagement among health care

professionals." Ohio State Journal on Dispute Resolution (2007)23(1): 105–142.

8. Weber, D. O. "Poll results: doctors' disruptive behavior disturbs physician leaders." Physician Executive (September/October 2004)30(5): 6–14.

9. Leape, L. L., and Fromson, J. A. "Problem doctors: Is there a system-level solution?" Annals of Internal Medicine (2006)144: 107–155.

10. Porto, G., and Lauve, R. "Disruptive clinical behavior: A persistent threat to patient safety." Patient Safety and Quality Healthcare (July/August 2006). Available online: http://www.psqh.com/julaug06/disruptive.html (accessed April 14, 2008).

11. Hickson, G. B. "A complementary approach to promoting professionalism: Identifying, measuring, and addressing unprofessional behaviors." Academic Medicine (November 2007) 82(11): 1040–1048.

12. Rosenstein, A. H. "Nurse-physician relationships: Impact on nurse satisfaction and retention." American Journal of Nursing (2002) 102(6): 26–34.

13. Hickson, G. B., et al. "Patient complaints and malpractice risk," Journal of the American Medical Association (2002) 287:2951–2957.

14. Hickson, G. B., et al. "Patient complaints and malpractice risk in a regional healthcare center." Southern Medical Journal (August 2007) 100(8): 791–796.

15. Stelfox, H. T., Ghandi, T. K., Orav, J., and Gustafson, M. L. "The relation of patient satisfaction with complaints against physicians, risk management episodes, and malpractice lawsuits." American Journal of Medicine (2005) 118(10): 1126–1133.

16. Gerardi, D. "The culture of health care: How professional and organizational cultures impact conflict management." Georgia Law Review (2005) 21(4): 857–890.

17. Keogh, T., and Martin, W. "Managing unmanageable physicians." Physician Executive (September/October 2004): 18–22.

18. ECRI Institute. Disruptive practitioner behavior report, June 2006. Available for purchase online: http://www.ecri.org/Press/Pages/Free_Report_Behavior.aspx (accessed April 14, 2008).

19. Kahn, M. W. "Etiquette-based medicine." New England Journal of Medicine (May 8, 2008) 358(19)): 1988–1989.

20. Marshall, P., and Robson, R. "Preventing and managing conflict: vital pieces in the patient safety puzzle." Healthcare Quarterly (October 2005) 8:39–44.

"Sentinel Event Alert" is © 2012 by The Joint Commission. Reprinted with permission.

Index

About the Authors

This is the second book by Steven P. Dinkin, Barbara Filner, and Lisa Maxwell. In 2010, they collaborated together to write *The Exchange: A Bold and Proven Approach to Resolving Workplace Conflict*. A third book applying The Exchange principles to community conflicts is in the works.

Steven P. Dinkin is the President of the National Conflict Resolution Center (NCRC). He has a law degree from George Washington University, where he taught a mediation clinic as an adjunct law professor. He has also taught mediation courses in the United States, Europe, and Latin America. For several years with the Center for Dispute Settlement in Washington, D.C., he served as an employment and workplace mediator for the Equal Employment Opportunity Commission (EEOC) and other federal agencies. In 2003, he moved to San Diego to lead the NCRC.

Barbara Filner was the Director of Training for the National Conflict Resolution Center (NCRC) from 1984 to 2010. She has a master's degree in teaching from Indiana University, and has worked as a teacher, a labor union official, and an analyst in local and state government. She has designed and conducted workshops on mediation and conflict resolution in the workplace in both the United States and Europe. She has lived in Pakistan, India, and Egypt, and thus brings a multicultural perspective to this book. She has also co-written two books about culture and conflict, *Conflict Resolution Across Cultures* (Diversity Resources) and *Mediation Across Cultures* (Amherst Educational Publishing).

Lisa Maxwell has been a mediator since 1985 and is currently the Director of the Training Institute at NCRC. She has extensive experience assisting groups dealing with conflict and managing other workplace disputes. She is the key person in the development of The Exchange Training. She has worked with large healthcare systems, the military, government agencies, and corporations in customizing the Exchange training for their organization.

About the National Conflict Resolution Center (NCRC)

The **National Conflict Resolution Center (NCRC)** has provided dispute resolution services nationally and internationally since 1983. Based in San Diego, California, NCRC is the largest full-service conflict resolution center in Southern California and one of the most prominent in the United States. NCRC demonstrates the ability to shift cultures through large-scale, high-impact, life-changing conflict resolution trainings. This dramatic impact is created through teaching effective communication and conflict resolution skills, which embrace collaborative teamwork and cooperation, benefiting healthcare systems, businesses, government agencies, and communities. With The Exchange in health care, NCRC's goal is to improve patient safety by bringing conflict management skills and strategies to the healthcare workplace by providing managers, supervisors, and HR professionals with a structured process to address communication issues and conflicts between their employees.

Discover unique solutions to managing conflicts and improve communication techniques within the healthcare industry.

the**EXCHANGE**®

strategies for managing conflict in healthcare

See what the Exchange can do for your healthcare organization.

- ■ Meets The Joint Commission's standards for healthcare improvement
- ■ Improves communication HCAHPS scores
- ■ Provides solutions for dealing with disruptive employees
- ■ Supports front-line staff working with patients

NATIONAL CONFLICT
NCRC
RESOLUTION CENTER

Approved Provider:
PHR, SPHR, GPHR

EACC Approved PDHs

Contact the National Conflict Resolution Center for customized trainings and trainer certification programs.

(619) 238-2400

ExchangeTraining.com